Ouainé Bain and Maureen Sanders work with children and young people who have been sexually abused. Ouainé Baine is a psychologist working for the Strathclyde Social Work Department and Maureen Sanders is an education worker, a member of the Overnewton Centre Project, specialising in the field of child sexual abuse. Frustrated by the lack of a good British book to give to teenagers they work with, they decided to write their own. *Out in the Open* is their first book. Friends for twenty-three years, they both live in Glasgow.

OUT IN THE OPEN

A Guide For Young People Who Have Been Sexually Abused

Ouainé Bain and Maureen Sanders

VIRAGO

Published by VIRAGO PRESS Limited 1990
20–23 Mandela Street, Camden Town, LONDON NW1 0HQ

Reprinted 1991

Copyright © Ouainé Bain and Maureen Sanders 1990

A CIP Catalogue record for this book
is available from the British Library

Printed in Great Britain by
Cox & Wyman Ltd, Reading, Berks

For our mothers
Dot Mitchell and Irene Sampson
and our daughters
Jenny, Chris, Helen and Emma

Acknowledgements

We would like to pay tribute to many others in Britain and the United States who have written in the field of sexual abuse and have provided valuable insights. We have drawn on many of those, in particular, *The Courage to Heal* by Ellen Bass and Laura Davis, and *Why Me* by Lyn Daugherty. Our 'Alert List' is a modified version of that used by the Sexual Assault Center, Seattle. We have benefited greatly from the published work of Lucy Berliner and the others at this Center, and from Lucy's visit to Scotland in 1987.

Warm thanks to colleagues, friends and loved ones old and new who have supported and encouraged us in this project, and to Judith, for precious and peaceful weekends in 'Fernachen'.

However, all of these people will understand if our greatest thanks are to the children, young people and adults who have trusted us enough to share with us their feelings, struggles and hopes – especially those who have contributed directly to this book in order to reach other victims. We feel very privileged to have provided a vehicle.

Contents

Use of Language

Throughout the book, we have used the masculine pronoun when referring to the abuser. This is because our knowledge at present is that the vast majority of abusers are male.

Some people feel that the word 'victim' is a negative label. We have used it in order to demonstrate that a 'victim' can become a 'survivor' when they have been enabled to take some control back into their lives.

Is this Book for Me?

Yes if . . .

- you have been, or think you might have been, sexually abused in the past

- you are being sexually abused now

- you feel you are in danger of being sexually abused

- you are aware of the publicity about the issue and want to get a clearer picture

- you are a parent, sister, brother, relative or friend of a victim of child sexual abuse and you want to be able to understand and help

- you are someone who works with children or young people and you want to be sensitive to the problem

- you are trying to offer help to young people (or adults) in working through the effects of child sexual abuse

To the Reader

We are really glad you have come across this book. We wrote it in the hope that there would be something in it that would speak to you. For those of you who are victims of sexual abuse we want to say that we know something of how you are feeling, and we want this book to help. For those others who want to give support to victims, we hope we are offering you some assistance.

We both feel very strongly that working with children and young people who have been sexually abused has been a learning experience for us.

We have learned, for one thing, that being locked in isolation and kept in ignorance breeds guilt, fear and helplessness. So we feel that it is very important that you have knowledge that will give you some control over the effects of your experiences. One of the first purposes of this book has been to gather together what we have learned and offer it to others in the hope that this will give you some strength and understanding.

We have also learned that there can be a terrible loneliness around sexual abuse. We hope that, in giving space to other people's stories and their account of the feelings they experienced, the book will help you to feel less isolated.

Included in this book are some suggestions as to what other victims have found helpful in their 'road to recovery'.

We know that reading this book will not solve all the problems, but we hope that in some way you find it helpful. We feel it is an optimistic book because one of the most important things we have learned from survivors is that, despite the pain, anger, fears and set-backs, it is possible to win through.

Section 1

Questions and Answers about Child Sexual Abuse

'The most surprising thing for me was to find out that sexual abuse really *happens* – and to lots of us – that it wasn't some weird thing that happened to just *me*.'

Jean, *Incest Survivor*

The following questions are some of the common ones asked by young people about sexual abuse. We have tried to answer them as best we can, based on our own experience and on the research that is being done in different parts of the world. But although sexual abuse is not new, the problem has come out in the open only fairly recently. So the answers to these questions will not necessarily be complete or satisfactory. They are based on our *present* knowledge and understanding.

What is sexual abuse?

Child sexual abuse happens when an adult or older person touches or uses a child in a sexual way. This can include different kinds of activities. But the main thing is, that by being bigger, stronger, or having power or authority in the victim's life, the adult can trap, lure, force or bribe them into sexual activity.

Why is it wrong?

It's wrong because it hurts the victim – sometimes physically, but more often psychologically. We know that it can cause confusion, fear, anger, shame, self-blame, and can leave the victim with a very poor opinion of themselves. Without help, the victim can sometimes have serious problems in later life.

It is wrong because everybody should have a right to decide what happens to their body. Adults should normally protect that right for children and young people. So any situation where physical force is used or threatened, or where the person feels they can't say no, can be called sexual assault. Children and young people, for many reasons, can't really say no to adults, nor have they the power to stop them. Young children do not even understand what is happening. The adult in this situation is always committing a crime.

12

How do I know if I have been sexually abused?

There are different things that can happen. Here are some examples:

Being:
- cuddled or kissed in a way that left you feeling uncomfortable
- bathed in a way that made you feel uneasy
- made to watch sexual acts or look at other people's genitals
- shown sexual films or videos, or being forced to listen to sexual talk
- made to pose for 'sexual' photographs
- touched on your breasts or genitals
- made to touch an adult's or older person's genitals
- made to have oral sex
- penetrated (having the adult thrust his finger, penis or an object inside the vagina or anus)
- raped (penetrated using force or violence)

There are other, less obvious things that may have been done or said to you that *you* have found abusive.

Is there any sexual activity in childhood that is okay?

When we talk about sexual abuse, we are not talking about children's 'sex play'. It is normal for children to touch their own bodies, or those of other children, in a way that makes them feel good. For them this is part of exploring and learning.

Nor are we talking about the kisses, cuddles and good touches that adults and children give each other. These are the ways we express affection, reassurance and caring for one another, and we do this in an open way. One of the ways of telling that the adult is making it a *sexual* approach is that he needs to make it a secret.

13

Are there really a lot of people who have been sexually abused?

Child sexual abuse has been taboo for so long and is such a secret crime that it is hard to find out how many people have been affected. Many more adults are talking now about their experiences and we are learning from them. Also there have been surveys done in many countries to try to estimate the problem. Although the figures vary, they all show that it is much more widespread than anyone realized in the past.

---

1 in 10

A Mori Poll in Britain questioned 2019 adults and found that 10% of them had had at least one sexually abusive experience before the age of 16 years – 12% of women (1 in every 8) and 8% of men (1 in every 12).

Of the 10%:

63% reported a single abusive experience

23% reported being abused repeatedly by the same person

14% reported multiple abuse by a number of people

Can sexual abuse happen at any age?

Yes, children can be sexually abused at any age, from infancy to adolescence. Between a quarter and a third of children who are known to have been abused are 5 years old and under.

The most common age for abuse to begin is 8–9 years.

Are boys as well as girls abused?

Yes. It used to be thought that many more girls than boys were abused. We now know that this is not the case. The difference in numbers between abused girls and boys is becoming less.

What about teenage sex?

We know that many teenagers are sexually active. In order to understand sexual abuse, it is important to work out what an acceptable sexual relationship is. We think it is between two people who agree to it, and where the partners are equal. It is wrong when one person *makes* the other agree to sexual contact – in any way.

This doesn't mean that, any time two people feel equal, it is necessarily okay to have sex. There are many different beliefs about when it is proper to have a sexual relationship, all influenced by religion, education and custom. As a result of these we decide with whom, at what age, and under what circumstances having sex is okay. Each person eventually has to decide for themselves what is right.

What other people have said . . .

'Sexual abuse is the betrayal of trust and the misuse of power.'

Suzanne M. Sgroi

'Incest is the sexual abuse of a child by a trusted adult in a position of power and authority over that child.'

Incest Survivors Campaign

'A child (anyone under 16 years) is sexually abused when another person, who is sexually mature, involves the child in any activity which the other person expects to lead to their sexual arousal. This might involve intercourse, touching, exposure of the sexual organs, showing pornographic material or talking about sexual things in an erotic way.'

Baker and Duncan

What different ways can sexual abuse happen?

To answer this question we think it would be helpful to look at sexual abuse under different headings.

One-off incidents

This type of sexual abuse occurs as an isolated incident. The abuser might be a stranger or someone you know. The abuse can include things like obscene phone calls, 'flashers' (men who expose their genitals in public places), and being 'touched up' in the cinema.

Rape and sexual assault

Clearly this is a much more serious type of one-off incident. Teenagers are more likely to be the victims than young children. With young children, penetration is usually in the context of a more long-term abuse, or on a rarer occasion, a child is abducted and raped by a stranger.

Although teenagers can also be raped by strangers, the majority of rapes (60% of those reported) are committed by someone known to the victim. And, in the main, this happens in places where the victims expect to be safe – for example, at home, at a friend's party, in a car with a boyfriend.

Victims of rape can be made to feel that they ought to have been able to avoid or prevent the attack. If this has happened to you, it is important to look at how rapists operate. They can use physical force or weapons, but they can also use more subtle methods which are designed to confuse you by making you feel that *you* are in the wrong or that *you* 'invited' his advances in some way. ('You weren't just asking me in for coffee, were you . . .'; 'I know what you really want . . .'; 'You've been coming on to me all night . . .') The attacker can take advantage of your confusion to get you into a situation where he can rape you.

Abuse that continues over a period of time

This is where the abuse may start gradually and can continue for weeks, months or years, because the abuser manages to avoid detection. He may be a neighbour who invites the child to his house to play regularly, or it could be a teacher, someone at a sports centre, or a family friend. They are often people who have made a point of being in a work or leisure situation in which they have access to children and young people. The victim may be a boy or a girl.

Sex rings and ritual abuse

It is known that children can be exploited by several adults who have formed a network or who live in the same community. (Or one adult can use an individual child in order to gain access to other children.) There is usually money involved. This kind of organization is referred to as a 'sex ring'. Children are no more responsible for this than they are for individual abuse.

We are also becoming aware that sexual abuse is part of the rituals of certain cults. These cults, which have as their central theme 'the worship of Satan', use particularly powerful methods to trap and silence children and young people.

Incest

In this type of sexual abuse, the abuser is a member of the child's immediate family, usually a step-father, father, grandfather or older brother. Because it happens within the family it is even more likely to be kept a secret and can go on for years. It can sometimes involve more than one child within the family. And, although in general girls are more likely to be victims than boys, both brothers and sisters can be abused in the same family.

What makes it possible for it to happen in the first place?

An older person always has greater power, authority or knowledge than a child or young person. He can exploit this difference in many ways. In the case of rape or violent assault, he can simply be bigger or stronger. But there are more subtle ways by which an abuser can involve a child. Sometimes he can use bribery – using gifts or special privileges. He can sometimes pretend that it is simply a game between them. He can lead a child to believe that the 'games' are normal or okay.

Does any of this sound familiar to you? . . .

'This is our little game . . .' 'I'll let you watch TV late if . . .'
'Come and I'll show you the tickling game . . .'
'You're my special girl/boy . . .' 'It's okay, everybody does it . . .'
'This is something special we do because we love each other . . .'
'I'll give you sweets/pocket money if . . .'
'I'll buy you a bike/puppy etc. if . . .'
'What's the matter? Don't you like me?'

The abuser is usually clever enough to make sure that no one else is around when these things are happening; and he usually starts it gradually so that the child is often confused about what is going on, and can become involved without really understanding what is happening.

Why is it so hard to stop it?

Children don't expect adults to harm them, especially those who take care of them, and are in a position of trust. And children are also taught, in general, to be obedient and to believe adults. So it is only too easy for an abuser to persuade the child that there is nothing wrong, and that they shouldn't tell.

At a later stage, victims don't tell because they are confused and afraid – afraid that they won't be believed; that they will be blamed or punished for what has happened; that the family will be broken up; that the abuser will harm them; that they themselves will be removed from the family or that something will happen to the abuser.

'This is our little secret. No one else will understand.'
'. . . nobody will believe you.'
'Don't tell your mother or it will make her ill/she will go away/she will be angry with you/she will kill you/she will kill me . . .'
'Don't tell or you will be put in care/I will be put in jail . . .'
'If you tell I'll just get another little boy/girl/I won't love you any more/I'll give you a doing/spanking/thrashing/I'll kill you/I'll kill your dog . . .'
'Everything will be all right if you just don't tell . . .'

Sometimes children and young people who are being abused feel they have tried to tell, by hints or clues, or something they have said or done. And sometimes they just feel that it must be obvious to others what is happening, especially if it is in the family. If no one appears to be doing anything to stop it, it can seem as if it is okay. The victim is further confused.

There is also the situation where, by going along with the abuse, the young person hopes that they can prevent sisters or brothers being abused. Finally, one of the saddest things about sexual abuse is that the victims may be silenced because they start to believe that somehow it is their fault, and this makes them take on the shame and guilt that belongs to the abuser.

So you can perhaps see more clearly why children and

teenagers sometimes work very hard to keep the secret, and why it is too frightening for them to speak out. Understandably, very few do tell.

One study has shown that the average amount of time that incest can go on before it is discovered is three and a half years.

Even those who have tried to tell are not always believed. They sometimes give up trying to tell anyone else.

'Don't worry about things like that . . .'
'Nice children don't talk about things like that . . .'
'Uncle Bob doesn't mean any harm – it's just his way . . .'
'How could you ever think such a terrible thing?'
'Don't let me hear you say anything like that again.'
'Where did you hear all this stuff?'

It is particularly painful for children if a *parent* does not initially believe them, and there can be serious, more long-term problems for the child if there *never* comes a time when they are believed and given support.

'How could you keep such a thing secret?'
'Why didn't you tell me . . . ?'
'Why did you wait until now if it really happened so long ago?'
'What are you trying to hide?'

Do other people know when it is happening?

From the victim's point of view, it often seems that others must know what is going on. However, abusers are usually very good at concealing from others the truth of what they are doing.

Often, when the abuse is on-going within the family,

it is very common for nobody to realize what is happening – even when the abuser is involving more than one member of the family.

Is the victim ever to blame for the sexual abuse?

NO! NEVER! . . . though they very often *feel* they are. The most important thing for people to know is that no one has the right to sexually abuse them, whether by force, or by taking advantage of their position. It is never the victim's fault, no matter what they do, and no matter what happens as a result of the abuser's behaviour. The abuser is totally responsible for his own behaviour.

Remember, it is never anything that the victim says or does that causes the abuse.

Nor is the victim responsible for anything that happens to the family or the abuser after they have told.

No Matter What You Said Or Did . . . It Was Not Your Fault!

Will the effects of this experience always be with me?

Different people are affected in different ways. This depends not simply on the abuse they have experienced, but also what help and support they have had to deal with it.

Victims have had to get themselves through some difficult and tough situations. Just managing from day to day has been an achievement. So they must have developed some important strengths.

However, the effects of child sexual abuse usually make their lives more difficult in some areas and these difficulties can be carried into adult life. Many times former victims do not realize that some of the problems they are having in their present lives are really the result of having been abused as children. Once they realize this, working out their problems becomes easier. Even those having more serious problems can usually benefit from professional help, or the help of other survivors, and they can greatly improve their lives.

Every Victim
Can
Be A Survivor!

Is it usually men who abuse children?

Yes. Men and older boys. It is known that the vast majority of offenders (about 97 per cent) are male. It is rare for women to abuse.

Are you more likely to be abused by a stranger?

Children are often warned about strangers. But in fact, if you have been sexually abused, it is more likely that it was by someone you knew. 80% of reported abuse takes place between the child and an adult *known* to the child. The person may have been a friend of the family, a baby-sitter, or a neighbour. Or it may have been an adult at school or at some kind of club or leisure activity.

Is it true that abusers are sometimes in the family?

It may be that you have been abused by someone who lived in the same house, or was very close to you. And you might have loved and trusted him. Many children and teenagers are abused by someone who is closely related to them, such as an uncle, cousin, brother, grandfather, step-father or father. And, although it is not very common, it may have been a female relative.

Is it possible to 'spot' an abuser?

There is no such thing as a typical abuser. They are mostly married men. They come from any age group. They come from every class, professional, racial and religious background. The person can seem very respectable on the outside and, at work or with friends, can seem to behave 'normally'. So you can see it is very difficult to 'spot' an abuser. As Michele Elliot, author of 'Kidscape', says: 'Molesters have only one certain characteristic – they molest.'

Why do people abuse children?

This is not an easy question to answer, but there are things we now know about abusers.

On the whole, they are people who need to have control, power or domination in their personal relationships – especially sexual ones. This need is not met satisfactorily unless the sexual activity is with someone they see as being in a much weaker position than themselves. Abusers have different ways of trying to meet their own needs. Some look for reassurance and acceptance from children and young people because they, the children, are trusting, can be manipulated and will not expect anything in return. Others are bullies, and just go for what they want.

Although their behaviour is abusive, inappropriate and harmful, very few abusers see themselves as having a problem. Most of them make excuses which help them avoid feeling guilty. For example, they say to themselves that they have a right to do what they like in their own families; that they are 'teaching' the victim about sex; that they are doing them a favour by introducing them to sex before 'any of these bad boys' do it; or that the sex is merely their way of showing that they care.

We know of a whole variety of these excuses – but that's exactly what they are – *excuses*.

> An abuser in long-term group therapy with other abusers said: 'We all knew what we were doing was wrong, but we each had stories we told ourselves, so we could keep on doing it.'
>
> *Working with Abusers*, Rick Snowdon

The main thing about abusers is that they are thinking only of themselves and not about how their behaviour might hurt the victim. In fact, abusers are very self-centred people who have trouble considering anybody's welfare but their own. Because *they* enjoy or need the sexual activity, they let themselves believe that the victims do as well. With some abusers, it is true to say that they just don't care whether they harm the child or not.

Even when the abuse is discovered, they will be anxious to put the blame on somebody else – on the victims, or on their wives or adult partner. They may say that the child 'led them on', or that they are sex-starved because their wives or partners are 'cold' or 'frigid'. Unfortunately, there have been plenty of people in our society ready to believe this in the past.

When there was little understanding about child sexual abuse, there were also theories that it happened because of other problems – alcoholism, money problems, violence or mental illness. We now know that, although these problems may or may not be around, they do not *cause* the abuse.

There was also the theory that the abuse occurred in certain kinds of families. But in fact it has been found in all kinds of families. (And anyway, this would not have explained the abuse that happened *outside* of families.)

Sexual abuse is a crime and abusers may have to go to prison. Whatever happens to them, it is necessary for there to be some controls, by outside authorities, on their behaviour.

Remember, victims should not feel responsible for

24

what happens to the abuser when the abuse is discovered. We do know that abusers almost never seek treatment voluntarily and that abuse will most likely continue, or re-occur with another victim, unless a report is made to someone in authority. Some abusers can be helped by treatment but this cannot really start until the abuser accepts *completely* the responsibility for what he has done, and the success of it always depends on how much the abuser wants to change his behaviour. Treatment is not easily available, takes a long time and requires a great deal of effort on the part of the abuser.

We know that most abusers have more than one victim. One study in the United States (Jean Abel and Judith Becker, Colombia University, New York) found that child abusers averaged as many as 73 victims before they were caught. It also revealed that a large proportion of people who abuse within their families also abuse outside their families.

Does any of this help us to understand why people abuse?

We believe that sexual abuse is not primarily a sexual problem but more a problem of the misuse of power. It has been found, when looking at the patterns of sexual abuse and the nature of abusers, that this way of looking at it makes the most sense. But perhaps this needs some more explanation.

We still live in a world that gives men permission to look upon women and children as their property. Society also makes men feel that they *have* to be dominant to be 'real men', and that women and children are not as important and should be, in some way or another, under their control. Men are supposed to be strong and powerful, women and children weak and submissive. Even though we know lots of people who don't fit into these

25

patterns, the myths are very strong and influence how we see ourselves in the world. (Boys and girls are taught this in all sorts of subtle ways, during their childhood.)

This can distort all our relationships in one way or another, and it means that when some men are threatened, or feel weak or powerless for whatever reason, they will often turn on someone weaker and use their sexuality in an abusive way in order to feel better about themselves.

You can see why abusive men cannot allow themselves to consider the feelings of the person they are abusing. They may say that the sexual activity is about loving or caring, but in fact it is really about satisfying their own needs.

Why me? Why did he have to do this to me?

We realize that this is probably the most painful question of all. Perhaps having read so far, you will understand that it was nothing particular about you that invited or caused the abuse. Unfortunately you were the one the abuser had access to, in circumstances he could exploit. This answer is probably as painful as the question, and you may need help to come to terms with this. We hope the rest of this book will help.

Section 2

Other People's Stories

'. . . to know I'm not the only person in the world.'

Liz, *member of a survivor's group*

The stories that follow have been written or told to us by people who have had different kinds of abusive experiences in their lives.

Some of them have told us how helpful it was for them to hear or read other people's stories. They have all agreed to contribute to this book in the hope that their stories, in turn, will help some of you to feel less isolated and lonely.

In all cases the names have been changed, not because these people were ashamed in any way, nor that they wanted to protect their abusers, but more out of consideration for others close to them.

Susan (age 30)

Strangely enough I had never talked to anyone about this incident until recently, but while I was telling a friend, I found myself shaking. It was something that happened when I was about 9 years old. We lived in a big house with a cellar where lots of stuff was kept for the kennels that my parents ran. I was swanning around there one Saturday morning still in my nightdress. Looking for something – I can't remember what. The man who worked in the kennels came in. I went across to talk to him. I quite liked him. He was kind of quiet and often let me help him. What happened then is hard to remember, but he had grabbed me and we were down on the floor and he was trying to hold me down and he was kissing me hard. I struggled and somehow got away and ran upstairs to my room. I was shaking like a leaf. I never told my parents. The man was highly respected in the village. I just went to great lengths not to go near him, and he left soon afterwards anyway.

Later I heard that he had got a job working for a residential school for difficult boys and had been charged with molesting them. By then I understood things a bit more, and I felt really guilty for not telling someone at the time. I might have been able to stop these boys being hurt like that. I still feel that.

James (age 28)

When I was about 13 or 14 years old, a few of us used to go away hill-walking with this guy. To us he was a real hero. He knew all about the hills. We used to take tents and camp overnight. It seemed like a great adventure.

Then it was my turn to share a tent with him and when we got undressed, he told me to masturbate him. He said he had shown all the others how to do this and it was okay. I felt trapped inside the tent and wanted to get away. But he had a way of making us want to please him, so I did what he asked. I never talked to the others about it, but I used to feel embarrassed that they knew. I carried on going out with him and the others for some time and taking my turn in the tent, until he started to do other things to me, and I found an excuse to drop out of the week-ends. I've always had real problems with sex.

Mhairi (age 18)

My early memories of my grandfather touching me seem to be about sitting on his knee in his big chair. We had this game about hiding sweets in his different pockets. I had to search in all of them, then he had his turn of 'searching' me, and that was when he would put his hand up my pants. It's hard to think now that I didn't dislike the game – there was a kind of excitement about it. Later on (I think) he took me into the bedroom, when my gran was out, to look for sweets. That was when he would take his trousers down and make me rub his penis. I couldn't understand what was going on, but I remember being really frightened about this – because he seemed to change and it wasn't a game any more. I can remember trying to stop my gran from going out to the shops, or I would ask if I could go with her.

I did manage to tell my parents in some way eventually, though I can't remember what I said. Everything seemed to be strained for a while and I remember my parents arguing and my mother crying a lot during that time. I didn't want to be left at my grandparents' house any more, and gradually I realized that I wasn't being taken there any more. But nobody had told me this for certain.

Soon after that we moved away and I didn't see my grandparents much after that – but I could never get over the feeling that I was to blame for the strain in the family and the fact that we were moving house. And I felt I had somehow turned my gran away from me and I had really loved her.

My parents never discussed the whole thing with me – not even when my grandfather died. I was older by that time but I remember feeling very strange when my mother was getting ready to go to the funeral. I think I felt I should be feeling sad – but I was feeling relieved and guilty at the same time.

Katy (age 12)

It happened usually when we came in from school – my sister and me. I can't remember what age I was when it started – it seems as if it always went on. He would get undressed and tell us to get undressed. Then he would touch us in our private parts and make us touch him. When I did it was all wet and sticky. He would never give us our pocket money until we had done this. Once I tried to push him away, and he slapped me on the jaw.

My dad didn't talk to many people, and he would never let us out to play so we didn't have any friends. My mum used to leave us a lot and go and stay at my gran's. I wanted to tell my mum but I didn't know how to do it. My dad said if I told anybody he would kill me. He said other people wouldn't talk to me and I believed him. It made me feel horrible and stupid. Once my little sister, Ann, and me were in bed talking about it and I decided to run away to my gran's and tell my mum.

But when I got there I got a row for coming out at night and my mum took me back home and had a row with my dad and I never got a chance to tell her. After that, we didn't know what to do.

How it all came out was that Ann was always in a real state in school – really nervous. I used to be really scared she would blurt it out to somebody, so I always stayed with her in the playground. My social worker told me that Ann started telling her teacher about her bad dreams and about monsters doing things to her and that's when they asked her questions about our dad. I was terrified when they asked me about it, but I'm glad now. We're in care just now and I never want to see my dad again, but I want my mum to get a house by herself and have us with her.

Hannah (age 16)

I had tried to tell my mum on lots of occasions about what had been happening to me but I never managed to get the words to do it. Then one morning about two years ago, it all came pouring out.

We had been talking about the past and my mum asked if I had any bad memories of my childhood. Straight away I thought about the things my uncle had done to me and the bad feelings that I still felt about what had gone on. But somehow I just couldn't tell her even then. I felt guilty and mixed up. I just pretended that I had to get something from my bedroom and said I would be back in a minute. I ran to my bedroom, shaking. I felt alone and weak – just as if I was a small kid again. There was a voice in my head saying 'You know you won't be able to tell her – he's got you beat again . . .' My mum came to my room, wondering what I was doing. I tried to hide the fact that I was crying, but then I just let go and told her everything that had happened. I can't begin to describe the relief I felt in telling someone. I still had, and do have, feelings of guilt and anger, but now there are people to help me sort these out.

I discovered then that my older sister was also sexually

31

abused by my uncle which made me even angrier with him. I knew the kind of feelings she must have had and somehow it was worse thinking about her being hurt in the way I had been. However, my sister and I are able to talk about it now and support each other and I don't think we've ever been closer. I still get upset about what happened, for example when I speak to my aunt who I have always been very close to. But instead of bottling up feelings, I can express them now. I feel stronger because I told and I didn't let him win in the end.

Jimmy (age 14)

I used to stay with my mum. I had a dad but I never knew where he lived and my mum would never talk about him. I was slow at school and was sent to a different school on a bus. The other kids used to slag me about this – they still do, but I can look after myself better now.

My mum had this boyfriend – this old guy – he came to our house every week-end. I was about 9 years old. I didn't like him much and he used to laugh at me. But I didn't get hit so much by my mum when he was around. Then worse things began. He started taking me into the bedroom when my mum was at the shops. He put vaseline on my bottom and stuck his willie in me. It was sore. I was scared to tell my mum in case I would get hit, and so I didn't know what to do. It happened a few times. Once my mum was in the house watching TV. I went and told her and she said not to bother.

How it all came out was that I was playing out the back with my pals and a big boy came and forced me to take my pants down and run into the street. They were all laughing at me. I was greetin' (crying) and somebody must have got the police. They asked me questions about what happened – then two social workers came to the house at night. They took me to the other room to speak to me away from my mum. I told them I didn't like Peter (mum's boyfriend). I was embarrassed to say what he did to me, but they let me whisper it. My mum wouldn't believe me. I wanted her to keep Peter out of the house, but she just kept getting mad at me.

The social worker put me in a children's home for a while. I didn't like it much – I wanted home to my mum's, but every time she came up to see me, we ended up shouting at each other. I'm with foster parents now and I like it fine.

Margaret (age 47)

I still remember the day vividly. I've worked it out that I was about 9 years old. It was a hot summer day during the school holidays. My older brother and his pal had let me tag along with them. We walked to some woods a couple of miles from our house. We were sitting having our crisps and lemonade when this man came along wheeling a bike. He sat down beside us and started talking. He suggested that we should 'go exploring' (I remember the phrase), but that the boys should go off by themselves and he would go with me. He became quite insistent and began pulling me by the hand towards some bushes. But I was crying by this time and saying I wanted to stay with my brother, so the boys followed us. Then he turned round and faced us, opened his trousers and pulled out his penis. It seemed enormous. He came towards me, telling me to hold it. We all turned and ran at that point. I can remember the feeling of my heart pounding, and we just kept running and running. We never told our parents and we never spoke about it between ourselves. I think we all felt we had done something wrong. It's something I've never forgotten though.

Molly (age 22)

It happened when I was 16. My parents were splitting up and I suppose I was looking for friendship and reassurance from people at that time. I met a man at a disco who seemed really easy to talk to. I immediately felt that I could trust him. When we got home I asked him in for coffee. I wanted some company because my dad was away and the flat was empty. At first he seemed happy just to sit and talk. Then he started to kiss me. I told him that I only wanted to talk. This made him suddenly very angry and he brought out a knife and held it at my throat. He forced me to lie on the floor and he raped me. It seemed to go on and on, and he was pushing things in me – pencils and finally a bottle. I couldn't scream. I thought he would kill me.

I don't know how long it went on for. I think I passed out and when I came to he was gone. I was very sore and bleeding heavily. I had a bath and then sat on my bed. I felt no emotions at all.

There was no bruising on my face so nobody noticed anything had happened. Two weeks later, I started feeling sick and discovered I was pregnant. I was so ashamed about the whole thing that I couldn't tell my mum and dad what had happened. I just said it had been a 'one-night stand'. I know I got a lot of support through the abortion that followed, but to be honest, I felt numb through it all. Looking back, I suppose I was still in a state of shock.

When I finally told someone I was so relieved that they believed me. I had a lot of terrible dreams – I still dream about it but less and less. I do find it hard to trust people.

I can talk about it more easily now. And I am convinced that he had no right to expect sex just because I had asked him in, and I had absolutely no reason to feel ashamed. Things are getting better . . . and I'm really glad to have written this down.

Janice (age 16)

My first memory of the abuse was my step-father being very tender towards me, and when he started touching me sexually, he always reassured me that it was all right for him to do this. I was old enough to know that what we were doing was wrong but I was too scared of him to be able to tell my mum. He had a really strong hold on me. He used to take me to school and bring me home. He even used to be in the park across from the school playground at breaktime watching out for me. I liked the attention in one way, but I didn't like the fact that it made me different from my pals.

He got more demanding and eventually he was having intercourse with me. When it got to this stage, he started making a real fuss of me. On the one hand, he restricted me from going out at night with my friends; on the other, he made me feel special, telling me I was his girl. I hated what he was doing to me but I liked being special.

It started causing real fights between my mum and him. Dad was always sticking up for me. It was as if in his eyes I could do no wrong. And this set my mum and me against each other. I used to have awful guilt feelings towards her. I tried time and again to tell her what was happening, but I could never find the words and I was afraid she wouldn't believe me – he used to say she wouldn't. I used to see the 'Childwatch' programmes on TV but I was too scared to phone. I couldn't wait to go to school in those days – it was as if I could just forget about everything there. I just bottled everything up till I went to bed at night. Then I used to cry and cry.

Then I got pregnant and I felt a terrible anguish about my mother and what she would say. I felt so guilty. Dad helped me make up a story and I just felt relieved that she believed it – even though it meant I took the blame. I went through the next stage – the abortion – feeling numb. My dad left me alone for a time and that was a relief, but it wasn't for long.

It got to the stage then that I just couldn't cope with things any longer and started running away from home. I told a friend what was happening because the same thing had happened to her and she helped me to go to the police.

After it all came out, there was a terrible time. My mum didn't believe me, and my dad denied everything. I hated him so much I wanted to kill him. I felt he had used me and had thrown away my life like a piece of rubbish. For my first four months in the Children's Unit, it just seemed to be hurt and more hurt from every point. My young brother and sister came into care as well and they blamed me for splitting up the family. Once my brother said he wished I was dead, and my mum was refusing to talk to me. I wanted to crawl into a corner and die. I thought nobody cared and nobody wanted to listen.

Gradually the people in the unit helped me through this. They started to reassure me, made me feel worthwhile again, and gave me confidence and a different kind of caring.

I got counselling from them which took some of the guilt and fear away, and eased some of the angry feelings between my family and myself. The abuse will always be there but I can see things in a different light now and I hope I can move forward.

Alice (age 48)

I lived next to a farm when I was young and spent all my time there. My home life wasn't much fun and there were a lot of rows going on. I always slipped out and escaped to the fields or the farm yard. It was my haven, I suppose. The farmer used to let me sit on his knee on the tractor when he ploughed, and later I got to drive it sometimes. I felt really proud to be able to help. And I loved the farmer's wife and the warm farm kitchen.

I must have been 11 or 12 years old because my breasts had just begun to develop. One day when I was hanging about as usual, the farmer made some teasing remark about this and grabbed me and rubbed them with his hands. His teenage son and one of the farm labourers were there and they all laughed.

All I remember after that was me running and running, with my face burning. I felt so ashamed and embarrassed and dirty. Although it wasn't a big deal really, it did have a lasting effect on me because something was spoiled then and I didn't go back to the farm much – and I really missed out on all the things I had taken refuge in.

Marion (age 17)

My father's side of the family always gave me a lot of attention when I was a kid because I was the only girl in the family (I had three brothers). My dad made me really special and used to call me his 'princess'. My mum left my dad when I was 10. She had tried to leave him several times, but he always came and talked her into coming back. I was always kind of glad because I was 'daddy's girl', but I know now that he treated my mum very badly.

From the time they split up, I went for summer holidays to my dad's – he had moved to a town on the coast and was living with another woman, June. The first year I went, he was the one who looked after me. He used to come in the bathroom when I had a bath, and he would say things like I would never have any boyfriends because I would always be his 'girl'. After that year, the touching began every time he put me to bed. I used to beg June to let me sleep in the same room as my little brother, but she always just agreed with what my dad said. After that he used to wait until she was out' and take me in the bedroom. By the time I was 14 he was having intercourse with me. Sometimes he used to call me by my mum's name when this was happening. He used to say horrible things about my mum at other times. I think he was getting back at my mum through me. I used to try to plead with him not to do it, and sometimes I tried to fight him off. I once threw a bedside lamp at him. He got quite nasty – I certainly wasn't his 'princess' then.

At the end of the holidays I used to plan how I would tell my mum. I didn't want to have to go back again the next time school holidays came. But I could never find the words and I couldn't bear to think how hurt she would be and what she would think about me.

I was a real problem in school – always in fights with teachers – and constantly in rows with my mother. I was seeing a school psychologist – and I used to long for her to ask me the right questions. But even when I took an overdose of my mum's pills and the psychologist came to see me in hospital, I still couldn't tell her about my dad. The worst thing was that when he heard about this, he came to see my mum and told her he would have me to stay with him so that she could have a break. I just remember sitting listening to him saying this and feeling desperate. And he carried on having sex with me even then. I finally managed to tell somebody just before the next school holiday. I was in this girls' group run by a social worker. We were all talking about subjects for discussion and somebody started talking about incest. I stayed behind that night and told the social worker that I thought that that was what was happening to me.

The worst thing was telling my mum. And then there was a bad time when the police said he would not be charged because there was not enough evidence! All his side of the family called me a liar and I never see them now. But I'm still glad I told. My mum and I are trying to work things out now. My main problem is not being able to eat much, and my mum worries about this.

Sonia (age 35)

My aunt used to come and babysit when my mum and dad were out. If they stayed out very late, she used to stay the night and she would sleep beside me in my bed. At first, I thought this was good fun and she used to read to me till late, and then cuddle up beside me. Then she started touching me and putting her finger inside me. I remember getting really scared at this – and it was sore. I asked her to stop, but she started saying she would tell my parents I was doing bad things, and that I would get the blame. And other times she would put on a kind of wheedling voice and say that what we were doing was okay, but that my parents would not understand. They were pretty strict so I suppose I was too scared to tell and I believed what she said.

Then it just seemed to stop and she would sleep on the couch if she stayed. But I was left with really dirty feelings about myself. And my aunt always seemed to have a hold on me. I always had to please her and do things for her in case she would tell my parents.

Scot (age 37)

I have a vivid memory of being out playing when I was about 10 years old. I had gone with an older boy from school. I thought of him as a friend. We were playing in a wood near our town. I'm not sure how it happened but he got me to take my trousers and pants down. He made me lie on the ground face down, and he held me down. I didn't know what was going to happen and I was feeling helpless and scared by then, but he kept saying I had to do it if I was going to be his friend. I could feel him trying to push something up my bum, but I was panicking and struggling. He got mad with me and went away. I lay there feeling humiliated. About the same time, I remember being taken to the doctor because of constipation, and I was terrified he was going to examine me. I don't know what I thought he would find out.

Much later, when I was about 14, a guy in the sports centre followed me into the toilets and offered me money to wank him. I didn't know what he was talking about at first. I got out, but I started thinking then that there must be something about me. I got quite depressed.

Moira (age 16)

My brother was 7 years older than me. I'm not really sure when it started, but it must have been before I was 8 years old because that was when we moved house and we were already playing the games by then. At first they were just about touching and I didn't think much about them. Besides he used to give me sweets and things. Later when I was about 11, he used to do stuff like holding me down and putting his penis in my mouth. He also pushed it in my vagina but – this might seem silly – I'm not sure if he was inside me or not. I was really scared of him by then and half the time I didn't know what was happening. I just seemed to cut myself off from it. He didn't always wait till my parents were out either. I used to be terrified that one of them would walk in – I felt I would get the blame. But by this time my brother was a real bully. When my dad was out, he used to intimidate my mum with his temper. She used to have to give in to him about things.

Then when I was 12, the sexual stuff stopped. I'm not sure why. But by this time I was really playing up in school. I was giving teachers cheek, and dogging (truanting). I got into sniffing glue and stuff with some other girls. The school brought in a social worker, and I could see that my parents didn't know what to do with me either. I just didn't care. Last year, I ended up going into a children's home. I met another girl there who told me she had been sexually abused by her father. It was then that I plucked up courage to tell my social worker.

I was lucky. My parents took my side. And my brother was put out of the house. At least he confessed to the police that he had done what I said. He is in a religious sect and apparently says he is all right because 'God has forgiven him'. That's okay for him, but I'm left carrying all the bad feelings.

I'm back home now and I feel like a different kind of person really. I get on with my parents, but I do worry about my mum. I think she feels guilty about my brother and I don't want her to have to feel that. I don't know what I would have done if my dad and her hadn't believed me and helped me.

I'm worried too about having to go to court – mainly about having to give evidence. You see though my mum knows what happened, I've never told her in detail and I'd die rather than say things in front of her. What will she think of me – she'll be disgusted.

Jennifer (age 23)

We lived in a flat when I was young. My little sister and I went through the usual craze of playing ball in the communal hallway with some other kids from the same flats. We must have been about 5 and 6 years old. One day when we were in the middle of a game, a man came in and asked us for directions. I don't remember now what he looked like, but I do remember that he said he had a cat and he needed to buy cat-food and wanted to know where the nearest shops were. We all spoke up, but I was a bit of a shy kid and I might have been hanging back. He lifted me up and asked if I would show him out of the window in the stairway. While I was doing this he put his hand up my pants and started to rub me. I don't think I shouted or anything – I didn't know what was happening, just that I wanted to get away from him. He put me down and went off. My main feeling was shame and embarrassment because I thought my pals had witnessed this. And I do remember that I never told my mum about it – and I usually told her about things that were bothering me. I must have felt it was something bad I had done.

Alison (age 17)

It all started when I was 12 years old. This old man was a neighbour and a good friend of the family. I used to go round to see him. Sometimes he would send me on messages and give me money. Then he started to feel me up and do all kinds of sexual things. He used to give me money for this as well, and told me not to tell anyone – not even my mum and dad. I thought it must be all right. I used to think it was because he cared for me and that I was supposed to do these things.

When we were in the top classes at primary school, my friends used to talk about boyfriends. I was really shy then, and didn't have anything to do with boys. But after the abuse started, I got involved in sex with boys because I thought that was what you did with boys. I got myself in a lot of bother. My parents tried to keep me in at nights – even locked me in – but I always got out. I started staying off school and running away, sleeping overnight with boys. Then I started to run away just because I couldn't cope with life any more. That's when I came into care. I gave them a hard time there. I was still running away, and I threw real temper tantrums – I got high as a kite for the slightest thing. I stayed out and ran around with boys.

I was still getting letters from the old guy, with money in them. One day after I got one of these, I ran away and when I came back I was feeling so bad about myself and I was sitting crying. One of the care staff asked me some questions and it all came out. I still don't think I could have told anybody if she hadn't asked. I don't even think I had connected up my behaviour with what had happened. I just knew I felt rotten.

Now I've had a lot of help from this person and I'm starting to believe in myself again. I've decided to stay in care. I have some contact with my parents – but my mum hasn't been able to say that she believes me or understands. I think my dad believes me now but he can't really talk to me about it.

Elaine (age 16)

I used to go with my family to visit my aunt sometimes in the holidays. We – my older brother and two little sisters – used to play outside with my older cousin. I can remember being really pleased when he said I could come into the shed with him one day. I usually felt the odd one out. I was a bit fat and I always thought nobody wanted to play with me. But this time he said no one else could come into the shed except me.

There was a lock on the door and he took the key in and locked the door. I thought this was part of the game. He lifted me up on a box. (I must have been about 7 years old.) Then he pulled my pants down and put his finger up my vagina – at least that's what I think he did. I had no idea what was happening at the time. I just knew it felt really funny and shivery and I wanted him to stop it. I remember he gave me a penknife that day and told me not to tell anyone. I think it was after we got home that my mother spotted the penknife and asked me where I got it. I lied right away and told her I had found it. I just remember feeling really guilty about having it.

After that it happened quite a lot, but by then my cousin was threatening to tell my mother about what I was doing in the shed, unless I went in there with him. I got so mixed up because I had started thinking I was the bad one.

So I started pretending to be sick when we were due to visit my aunt – and I really did seem to develop a lot of health problems at that time.

Donald (age 16)

Have you ever thought what it must be like to be sexually abused by someone in your family? I can tell you. It makes you feel crazy. It makes you want to kill yourself.

I was abused by my father from the age of 8 up to last year. It started out of the blue when he was mad with me one night. He took me up to the bedroom. I thought I was in for the usual leathering but this time when he took my pants down, he abused me with his prick instead. When he was finished, he said that's what I would get if I didn't do what I was told. I thought it was some weird kind of punishment.

As I got older, I became a loner and got myself into lots of trouble – shop-lifting, staying off school. I used to hope I would get caught and every time I was, I would long for them to put me away – in care, in a children's home, I didn't care where I went. But they never did. You see I haven't told you the worst. In the middle of this, my mother died. I discovered last year when it all came out that my father had been abusing my two big sisters for years – even while my mum was dying. And there's more to come. Maybe the thing that hurts me most. A couple of years ago, he started getting my older brother to abuse me. I tried to kill myself twice last year.

Now that it is out and we have been to court and he's in jail, I don't want to die. I want to live for my mother's sake. I'm getting some help and I'm relieved that it's over. But I'm still full of anger and hate for him and for my brother. I know he was abused himself – but that's all the more reason he shouldn't have done that to me.

Section 3

Telling

'We are not going to keep men's secrets any more. It's time we all spoke out.'

Survivor, *'Crimes of Violence'*, *Channel 4 TV*

Breaking the silence

Child sexual abuse thrives on silence and secrecy. Breaking that silence is the most important step in your recovery. No matter how hard you try, it is extremely difficult to stop abuse or to recover from it on your own. For those of you who are dealing with abuse that happened in the past and may have been a one-off incident, it is still important to be able to tell somebody about it.

Why tell?

- you move away from the guilt and secrecy that keeps you isolated
- you make it possible to get help to stop the abuse
- you make it possible to get understanding
- you may prevent it from happening to other children
- you start to get back some control in your life
- you join up with other young people who are no longer willing to suffer in silence
- you help other young people to tell

We have already talked about some of the things that make it hard to tell, and we know that some of you will have tried unsuccessfully to tell, through your behaviour or by indirect hints. But, if you haven't already done so, now is the time to find the words and to find the person to tell. It is going to be a scary business, and it won't always work the first time. Don't give up. Although it will be hard, you need to find somebody who will believe you and help you stop the abuse. In Section 7 we talk about some of the professional people who can do this. But you might want to start off by telling somebody who could help you to approach them.

Finding the words

No one is practised in talking about sexual matters. Here are some ideas:

- decide how much you want to tell before you start
- think out in your mind some sentences you might use to tell
- write these down, or . . .
- rehearse in front of a mirror, or . . .
- use a tape recorder, or . . .
- talk to someone on a phone line (see Section 7)

REMEMBER: It is your *right* to tell. *No one* has a right to sexually abuse you.

What happens and who is involved?

We can't tell you precisely what will happen when you tell, but we can give you a broad outline of what to expect.

Social workers are the people you are most likely to have contact with if sexual abuse is reported. They have a duty as part of their jobs to protect children and young people and keep them safe. (In Scotland, the *Children's Panel*, advised by the *Reporter*, is part of this process.) In making sure of this, they might be involved in supporting parents (who have not been involved in the abuse), or another adult, in caring for you, or they might arrange for you to be in care – perhaps in a children's home, hostel or with foster parents.

Whoever the person is who you tell about the abuse, they may well report it to a social worker. In fact, many professional people who have contact with children are instructed to report concerns about child abuse to Social Work Departments (Scotland) or Social Services (England, Wales and Ireland). So, for example, if you talked to a teacher, school nurse or a residential worker, they would be obliged to report this, although they would probably prefer instead to help you to do this.

A medical examination is sometimes necessary during an investigation. This can be in order to get evidence, but it can also be to check that there is no damage or infection. This will be done by a *doctor* – possibly one that you don't know.

Sexual abuse is a crime, and the *police* are required to investigate it. In some areas, there are police who are specially trained to do this. They are often police women. This will mean them asking everyone involved questions.

Telling about sexual abuse does *not* always mean you have to go to *Court*. But there are two situations in which you may have to appear as a witness. One would be when your care and protection is the issue, and the Court (and the *Children's Panel* in Scotland), has to judge how best to keep you safe.

The other is when there is a criminal charge against the abuser and you are a witness as to the crime that has been committed. This kind of court appearance happens less frequently. Sometimes a case cannot even be brought to the criminal court because, under our legal system as it is at present, there needs to be evidence that backs up the child/young person's statement. This can be in the form of medical signs, a witness who was present at the time of the abuse, or, in certain circumstances, the evidence of someone else abused by the same person. Because sexual abuse is such a secret, and because there are seldom lasting medical signs, you can see how difficult it is to bring an abuser to justice.

If an abuser *is* found guilty, it is the judge who decides on his sentence. This has been found to vary enormously ranging from fines or probation to prison sentences of different lengths. So it is difficult to get reliable advice about what will happen to an abuser within the legal system.

We know that in the past the process which a young person has to go through following a report of sexual abuse has not always been handled well. But most professional people are trying to learn more about children who are abused, and, in the process, are becoming more sensitive.

But however sensitive they are, it is a difficult time for victims. We would like you to make sure that you have someone with you who is going to help you to ask the necessary questions of all these different people so that you feel you have some control over what is happening and you are properly prepared for the different stages. In particular, the thought of being a witness in court is always an especially frightening prospect, and there are ways in which you can be helped to prepare yourself for this.

Surviving the crisis

Once the secret is out, there is often a period of crisis and upheaval and this can be a frightening time for you. The kind of support you get from your family is crucial. But the abuse may affect all the family members in one way or another.

They will often experience the same kind of emotions as you – confusion, fear, anger, shame, guilt. Parents may blame themselves for not preventing the abuse. Family members are often very angry with the abuser, or they may even blame you for what has happened. Seeing other members of the family upset like this will make you feel worse. You might draw back from talking about it to them for fear of upsetting them even more. Or they might be too embarrassed or frightened to talk about it, and may want to sweep it under the carpet.

We hope you will be lucky enough to have people in your family who will reassure you and support you. Even if you do, it is also good to have help from professional people through this crisis time, and it can help to know that the others in the family are getting that support as well.

If the abuse has been within your family, the opening up of the secret can result in feelings and reactions that can be quite overwhelming, and everyone needs help. There may well have to be some big changes in the family before the abuse can stop. We think that the best thing is if the abuser is out of the home. However willing he is to change his behaviour, and however much help he is going to get, you are not going to be safe during this time if he is still around. But you might find that, in order to get that protection, you have to spend some time out of the home – perhaps in care. This can be a nightmare time with a lot of pressures on you. So much so that you may begin to wish you had never told in the first place.

REMEMBER: Your family members may need time to sort out their feelings. If they are not giving you the support you deserve now, it may be because they need some help themselves.

REMEMBER: Whatever has happened as a result of you telling (even if it involved the abuser being punished) it is his responsibility – NOT YOURS.

DO:

- remember you are not going crazy. You are not mad and you are not bad. To have got this far you are courageous and strong
- try to talk to an adult you can trust about what is troubling you *most* at this time. It could be that you need help to deal with family reactions, or you could be worried about what is happening to the abuser, or you could be wanting to feel safe
- ask questions of any professional people involved about what is happening and what decisions are being made
- take one day at a time

DON'T:

- be tempted to say that it was all lies in the first place. *However many pressures are on you at this time, you are right to stick to the truth.* You owe it to yourself
- hurt yourself. If you feel suicidal and can't get help from the people around you – try one of the phone-lines (Section 7)
- despair. This time will pass. Each hurdle you overcome is making you a stronger person

Reporting rape

These are just a few important points. You will find useful information and advice on pages 81–90 in *Too Close Encounters – And What To Do About Them* by Rosemary Stones. (Listed in Section 7.)

- Following a rape attack you will be in shock. However stunned you feel, phone or go for help *immediately*.
- Contact your parents or a friend, and, where possible, Rape Crisis (phone numbers in your local directory).
- If you can't get a hold of anyone, or if you prefer, ring the police directly.
- In order to be most effective, the police need to know about an attack as soon as possible after it has happened.
- Even though the police are becoming more sensitive in interviewing rape victims, some of the questions they ask may make you feel somehow to blame. That's one of the reasons it's good to have someone with you.
- Until you have made contact with the police, don't wash, change your clothes or take drugs or alcohol.
- The police may want to arrange a medical examination in order to get evidence and to advise you on any further medical treatment you may need.
- Do your best to describe everything that happened during the attack, even though you might not know the 'correct' words.

REMEMBER: Although the main reason for reporting an attack is for your own satisfaction, you may be providing vital evidence that will prevent your attacker raping others.

Section 4

Feelings

'Sometimes I had so many different feelings churning around in my head that I wanted to hide in a corner somewhere and close my eyes, put my fingers in my ears and shut out the whole world.'

Moira's story

Where are you?

Are you:
- not sure if what's happening is, or is about to be, sexual abuse?
- becoming aware of unsettling memories?
- currently being abused?
- dealing with the effects of long-term abuse suffered in the past?
- dealing with the effects of a single incident?

Are you:
- still trapped in the secret?
- trying to find ways of telling?
- dealing with having tried unsuccessfully to tell?
- dealing with having told someone recently, but being disbelieved or ignored?
- in a crisis situation following the abuse coming to light?
- going through the process of coming to terms with abuse, with or without help?

Feelings

Other people's stories will have given you some idea how they felt at different stages. Whatever stage *you* are at, you will have experienced powerful and often confusing feelings. These feelings will have affected you in many ways, and may have influenced how you think about yourself and how you act.

It is common for victims to experience some psychological distress. Each person is different in how they react. Each situation is different. How bad the distress is for you will depend on several different factors. For example, what age you were when the abuse occurred; how long it went on and what was involved; whether it was a person within the family (or somebody close that you trusted), or a stranger. Most importantly, how well you cope with and recover from the distress will depend on how much support and understanding you get from family members or the people you turn to for help.

Joan's parents believed her when she told about her older brother abusing her. 'I just can't imagine what it must be like if you are not believed. It must be like being down a big hole fighting to get out and having people pushing you back down . . .'

In this chapter, we would like to look at the different feelings that you have and how they might have affected your behaviour. As you read you might find yourself recognizing some of them. We hope that we will help you to understand that these are *normal* reactions to sexual abuse, and that you are not alone in feeling them. We feel that, by doing this you will be making important steps towards recovery.

Rape Victims may find that they experience similar feelings to those discussed here. If this has happened to you, you may recognize many of them, particularly fear, anger, self-blame and depression.

Confusion

This is perhaps the best way to describe your state of mind when sexual abuse first happens. There seems to be no way of figuring out what the experience is all about. 'What is happening? Can it be okay for this person to be doing this? Why do I have these strange feelings? What is going on? Why is it a secret? Will it happen again?'

Jill was abused by her step-father from the time she was 6 years old: 'When it began, he said it was games and I thought it was sort of natural, you know. I just thought it was something that dads did. I'd never known my own dad.'

Gillian: 'He would come in the room at night to tuck me in bed and would put his hands up my nightdress. Because he was my mum and dad's best friend – he came to our house every weekend and went to the pub with my dad – I thought they must know what he is doing so they must think it's okay.'

Jan, to her mother after it had come to light that her 'favourite uncle' had abused her as a small child: 'But at the time I think I assumed you must know about it and that, because of that, it was okay. Remember the photos of me sitting on his knee. I thought when we looked at that photo, you knew what was going on.'

It is natural to be confused when something happens that you don't understand. You can't be expected to know how to respond to sexual abuse. The abuser uses your confusion to take advantage of you, and, by making it a secret, cuts off all the normal routes you would take to get some of your questions answered and your confusion reduced.

Joanne: 'From the start he told me that it was a secret and if I said anything mum would send me away. But I should have known he was tricking me. I suppose I was scared of him too. He used to flare up a lot and was on drugs – but still I can't help thinking I should have told my mum.'

Because sexually abused children and young people have been introduced to sexual activity in a totally inappropriate way, they are often confused about how to act with other people.

Sally: 'My dad said you only do this with me and nobody else. But when the boys started paying attention to me in secondary school, and asking me out, I didn't know what to do. So I did the same sexual things.'

When an experience is confusing and painful, and there seems to be no way of explaining or understanding it, we often cut ourselves off from it and bury it in our minds. If the abuse has continued over a period of time (or if you are dealing with abuse that happened in the past), you may have very hazy memories of how it began and of what has happened. This can lead to further confusion as to what part you might have played in it, and what has actually happened to your body.

Even after a victim has grown up, some confusion about the sexual abuse may remain. That is why it is important for you to learn as much as possible about child sexual abuse, and maybe find the answers to the many questions you have lived with for so long.

Along with the confusion about the sexual abuse comes the confusion about the many different emotions you feel at different times.

Liz's grandfather abused her regularly over a period of time: 'He was a real Jekyll and Hyde character. As nice as ninepins in company – full of treats for his grandchildren – he even played Santa once at a party in the local community centre. I loved him when he was like that and felt proud of him. But when he had me on his own and wanted sex, he was totally controlling and impatient and wouldn't listen to me. I got so confused. It was like dealing with two different people.'

And the trouble is that, although many of these emotions seem to contradict each other, you can seem to be feeling them all at the same time. They can leave you frightened, ashamed, or exhausted, and the resulting confusion makes you unable to deal with the other bits of your life – school, homework, friends, and so on.

Fears

Victims of sexual abuse have many things to fear. The sexual abuse itself is something that may be very frightening particularly if the abuser causes physical pain or threatens the victim. Both before and after abuse has been found out, the victim will be in a state of fear about where and when it is going to happen again.

Mary was one of three sisters who managed to fight off most of her father's advances because they would help each other out: 'So when my older sisters left home, I went to bed every night with all my clothes on.'

You may be afraid that you have been physically hurt or that people will regard you as being 'damaged goods'.

Moira's abuse by her older brother included at least attempted penetration before it stopped when she was about 11 years old. She is still not sure what happened, and has worries about her body: 'I have very painful periods. I keep thinking it might have something to do with what my brother did.'

Sharon: 'When I was with friends in school sometimes I would think: "If they knew they wouldn't be talking to me like this – they wouldn't want to know me".'

June, a victim of rape: 'It took me a long time to realize that I could tell friends about it and they wouldn't think I was contaminated in some way. I suppose that's how I was feeling about myself really.'

Victims may fear that if they try to tell someone of the abuse they will not be believed, or that they will be blamed and perhaps punished.

58

Richard remembers his Sunday school teacher regularly taking him into the toilet at the end of the class where he was made to fondle his penis: 'He told me that if I didn't keep quiet about it, it would go into a report to my school and it would go in my records that I was bad and all my teachers would know.'

Zahida: 'I wanted to tell my gran but I couldn't find the right words, and I knew he would be able to say it better than me, so everybody would believe him.'

On the one hand they may be afraid that the abuser will harm them if they tell. On the other, they may be afraid about what will happen to the abuser, especially if he is someone they love or are dependent on.

Joe: 'He threatened if I talked he would give my mum a beating and he would have – he'd done it before.'

Gerry feels very bad about the fact that he wasn't able to blow the whistle on the family friend who abused him. He feels he could have prevented his younger brother being abused also: 'He told me that he would put poison in my dad's tea and would stab my mother and my dog would go missing. I can't believe I was daft enough to believe him.' Gerry was 6 years old when the threats were made.

Debbie is 3 years old. She told her mother after it was discovered that her father was abusing her on access visits to his home, that he had threatened to get 'another little girl' if she told her mum.

Laura, raped by her mother's boyfriend, was told that he would set his dog on her if she told anyone. It was a heavy bull mastiff, 'trained for hunting and making a slow kill'.

Daniel, a 5 year old boy anally abused by his uncle: 'Oh no. I can't tell you who the monster is. He's got a knife and he can cut your head off.'

Moira finally told about her older brother's abuse of her:
'When they came to ask my brother questions, he made out
as if it had only happened once, then he was shouting and
bawling at me that I was a cow and that I'd asked for it.
Then he was sitting counting out tablets in front of my mum
and dad and saying he was going to take an overdose. I was
just standing there feeling terrified about what I had done.'

There are fears for the victim associated with having to
talk to lots of different people about the abuse, and of
course the idea of testifying in court carries with it a
whole range of anxieties.

Victims can be afraid that the family will break up as
a result of them disclosing the abuse. They can be afraid
that their brothers and sisters will be angry with them or
that they will lose the love of the abuser or of their
parents.

There are so many fears around that the victim might
end up being fearful all the time, without being able to
identify exactly what it is that is causing the fear. We
sometimes call this an 'anxiety state' and it is a very
common response to sexual abuse.

Michelle: 'I had one friend in school and she used to say I
was "jumpy" and I suppose I was. I used to get the slightest
thing out of proportion – things that she seemed to take in her
stride. I even felt I couldn't breathe properly sometimes.'

Joan wears layers of clothes – often big baggy jumpers –
even in hot weather. She regularly wears several pairs of
pants. 'My clothes are my armour.'

Teresa, a rape victim: 'I can't be alone in the house with a
man now – even someone I like.'

If you have experienced any of these fears you may have
been able to talk about them, but they may also have

been expressed in recurrent nightmares, disturbed sleep, bed wetting, eating difficulties, running away, and in being unable to concentrate, particularly in school.

Gillian: 'It got to the stage when I couldn't stand being in school – I felt closed in and I couldn't follow what was being taught. I started staying off, and just wandered around by myself.'

Ronnie: 'I got so desperate, I kept running away from home. I had to get out – and I suppose I was trying to draw attention to myself – it seemed like the only thing to do.'

Doreen, to her helper: 'I have this dream where we are in a graveyard and I'm feeling very scared. I try to calm down but it's not working. I see this man coming towards us with no face. I just see his hands. I shout for you and nobody comes. Then I'm struggling to get away.'

Manjit: 'I always have this dream where I'm running and he's running after me and I'm trying to get away. And sometimes when I shut my eyes at night, I see his face coming towards me.'

George: 'I have terrible difficulties sleeping – especially if my brother is away and I'm in the room by myself. I need to leave the door open so that I can see the light from the living room. The minute I shut my eyes, my mind starts playing tricks. I see these faces and they are all moving towards me, and when I open my eyes they are all over the walls. Sometimes I lie awake till about four in the morning until I'm exhausted. Then when I do sleep I have these dreams. It's always faces – though sometimes I'm looking at the backs of the heads and they turn round and they are horrible faces.'

If your anxiety has been extreme, you may have found yourself acting like a small child in some way. You may even still be finding this. Remember this is just a way of expressing a fearful state.

Guilt and shame

We have talked in Section 1 about the helplessness of a child/young person in an abusive situation and the secrecy that surrounds it. At first, the victim is keeping the secret because of confusion and, sometimes, fear. They feel helpless – powerless to stop the sexual advances of an adult. If the abuse continues, however, in order to find a way of living with it, the victim adjusts to it and is trapped by it. One of the ways you might have found of doing this is to believe that you are the guilty person – that you are responsible for the abuse. The fact that you somehow went along with it and didn't tell means, in your mind, that you must carry some of the blame. Also, it is too frightening for you to think of a known and trusted adult (especially if it is a parent) doing something wrong to you, so you are forced to think of yourself as the bad person. 'It must be something about me', 'I must have asked for it.' For those of you who have been abused by more than one adult, that feeling is even stronger.

The fact that there were parts of the abuse that you might have found in some way pleasurable, or that the abuser gave you special rewards either in the form of gifts or attention, only reinforces feelings of guilt. You may feel guilty, too, about any good feelings towards the abuser or, on the contrary, for wishing him dead, or for bad feelings towards family members who were not helpful enough.

If the abuse is within the family, you may feel responsible not just for the abuse, but for the emotional well-being of the family. It becomes your duty to keep the secret in order to keep the family together, or to protect the abuser.

Margaret: 'My dad kept telling me that I should stop him. He kept saying it was wrong and we would both get into trouble and that I must stop him. I tried to do this – but it made no difference. It was just as if he didn't hear me.'

If you finally manage to tell about the abuse, the relief can be great, but it can be accompanied by further guilt. You may feel responsible for many of the things that happen then – family break-up, public humiliation, possible criminal charges on the abuser.

Above all, in opening up the secret, you may feel you have exposed your own guilt and shame, and will have fears that people will find you unlikeable, 'dirty' or even disgusting.

During an investigation of sexual abuse, the victim's guilt feelings can be made worse in many ways. They can be reinforced by the abuser's downright denial, or by his shifting of the blame on to the victim.

Jill: 'I had two abortions before I was fourteen, and my father kept telling social workers that I was out of control, and was staying out late and had all these boyfriends. If they'd only known – I was never allowed outside the door after school and I was totally at his beck and call.'

Tahira: 'He kept saying "You like this, don't you. You want it."'

There may be sisters and brothers who do not understand and may blame the victim for the disruption of the family. And, particularly if the abuse involved the father (or mother's partner) there will be complicated guilt feelings towards the mother.

Sometimes the guilt feelings are so overpowering after the victim has told that it becomes easier to take back what has been said. This often happened with victims in the past. People in authority are becoming more sensitive about the victim's feelings and are realizing the role that guilt plays in keeping the victim quiet. We believe there is now a greater willingness to believe the child's story, and an understanding that helplessness, secrecy and an inability to tell are the *normal* reactions of *normal* children to sexual abuse.

Although guilt and feelings of self-blame are particularly associated with long-term abuse within the family, we are sure you will recognize these in most kinds of abusive situations.

Anger

Victims of sexual abuse have many good reasons for being angry. It may be that you are angry with a number of people, too. You may be angry at the abuser because of what he has done, and at his denial, both during and after the abuse.

Jane, of her father who abused her: '*If something came on TV about sexual abuse, he had the hypocrisy to sit there and make comments about how disgusting it was and how the people who did it should be locked up. I couldn't believe it. I was so angry but I couldn't do anything about it. I wanted to shout and scream right there in the living room.*'

If the abuser was someone in the family, you may feel angry with your mother for not knowing what was going on and therefore not protecting you from the abuse. You may be angry with sisters and brothers because they 'escaped' the abuse. You can also be angry with them if you find that they were abused and you had been led to believe you were 'special'. Or perhaps, by being the one that was abused, you were protecting them from it. (Abusers are very good at driving wedges between victims.) If you have talked to someone outside the family about the abuse and they have not believed you, you may be angry with them too.

Because helplessness is at the core of sexual abuse it can be particularly difficult for children or teenagers who are victims to express their anger. Often they are afraid of what will happen if they do. Will the abuser punish them? Will their mother reject them? Will they find that, if they unleash their anger, it will be so strong that they will do something violent to the person they are angry with?

Catherine was abused over a long period of time by her father: 'I used to feel so murderous about him that I carried a knife about with me. Then when I saw him in court, I was really worried about him because he had a heart condition. It was still me being sorry for him even though he sat there and denied everything.'

Joan: 'I hated my brother so much. I used to go into his room at night when he was sleeping and just stand over him with my fists clenched wishing I could kill him.'

For someone who has been powerless, anger itself can be such a terrifying prospect that it has to be 'repressed' or directed inwards. The victim who is outwardly passive and anxious to please can be inwardly seething with anger and hostility. Because it has no outlet, this rage can show itself in depression or withdrawal, in physical symptoms (headaches, vomiting, and so on), or in aggressive dreams and fantasies. The victim can find themselves lashing out at others for no apparent reason, and, most tragically, can inflict physical hurt and injury to themselves.

Feeling different

You may have found that part of being a victim is feeling 'different' from other people. You may feel that you are the only person that this has happened to. This leaves you feeling isolated and, even in a social situation, often very lonely.

Feeling 'different' usually means feeling dirty, worthless, or 'contaminated' in some way, and victims have told us about their fears that people, even by just looking at them, will be able to tell that they are 'different'. Because of these feelings, you may have 'chosen' to isolate yourself, cutting yourself off from friendships that may well have offered some support.

Rachel: 'I used to have three showers a day, and still I felt I had a smell.'

Pat: 'I made every excuse under the sun to avoid P.E. I just couldn't bring myself to change in front of other girls. I thought they would see that I was dirty.'

Claire: 'Every time he came to my room, I would lie rigid and pretend to be asleep. I think I felt that if I did this nothing would happen. But also it helped me sort of cut myself off from what was happening. I ended up feeling like a zombie most of the time.'

As we have said earlier, it is rare for women to sexually abuse, but for that very reason, young people who have been abused by women might feel very different and particularily isolated. Whereas most of the feelings we are discussing in this Section apply equally to all victims, we realise there may be some unique problems for you if you have experienced this.

One young woman has told us about feeling the lack of boundries between her and her abusing mother. She feels somehow taken over by her, and that her mother controls her thoughts even. Another adult survivor has stated how much she hated growing into a woman because it meant looking like (and becoming) her mother. These are two examples and we are conscious that neither of them apply to male victims. We have little information about particular problems boys might have in this situation.

Worthlessness

Earlier we talked about how some victims can feel responsible and guilty about what has happened, can feel they are 'damaged goods', and imagine that no one could possibly like them if they knew what they were really like. All of this will undermine any good feelings you might have about yourself. 'I'm worthless . . . I'm nothing . . . I'm dirt.'

Rose was raped when babysitting for a friend: 'I put bleach in my bath water to try to get clean again.'

Joan was abused by her step-father: 'I got really depressed, and stopped bothering about myself. I never washed my hair or anything. I even stopped cleaning my teeth. I think I was trying to make myself so horrible he would get put off and not try anything again.'

The chances are that you will have little confidence in yourself. Socially you may well feel you don't *deserve* anything good from anyone.

Richard: 'I was sick and frightened every time – and yet I felt as if I deserved it because I wasn't strong enough to do anything about it.'

Many victims begin to hate everything about themselves and describe their physical appearance in derogatory terms. 'I'm fat . . . I'm ugly . . . I'm skinny . . . I'm unattractive.' Some find themselves so unappealing that they will get into sexual relationships to prove to themselves that they are 'desirable'. Often they are exploited in the process, thus reinforcing their own feelings of worthlessness.

Sadness and depression

These are also common feelings experienced by victims. You may have felt sad and despairing. It may be that you have found yourself crying without really knowing why. All you know is that you feel empty and lonely. Crying can be a way of relieving those very natural feelings. You may have expressed your sadness in a physical way – by being tired or physically ill. The despair that is at the heart of the depression may have been so bad that you have hurt or mutilated yourself, or wanted to die.

Kirsty: 'I took overdoses – three times – and when someone found me each time, it just didn't matter to me because I was dead inside.'

Laura: 'I tried to cut my wrists twice before anyone knew about what had been happening. I was in care at the time. Then I just thought why should I do it – I've got things to live for really – I felt it was him who should do the dying.'

June, when she is really low, cuts her arms. 'To be honest, I feel better afterwards – it seems to let all the bad out: And the physical pain seems to stop the pain inside my head.'

Mixed up in this may be strong feelings of loss. You have, after all, lost many things. You may feel you have lost the love of important people in your life; you have lost the security of being able to trust adults; and in many ways you have lost out on your childhood. These are frightening losses and it is no wonder that it can feel like grief.

Life must be pretty tough for you if you are going around with all of these feelings – or even some of them. Just reading this chapter may have left you feeling upset. It may not be possible for you to deal with all of this on your own, so it is a good idea to get some help. Later in the book we will be talking about some of the things you can do to help yourself, and some of the people who might be able to help victims become survivors.

Section 5

The Road to Recovery

'By now, that darkness was no longer a deep well out of which I didn't know how to climb. It was more like a night that I knew would, in time, pass into day.'

Jacqueline Spring, *Cry Hard and Swim*

Will I ever be okay?

You may be feeling right now that your problems are so big that nothing and no one can help you, or that you will never be okay again. We know of many young people who have felt this way, but who have been able to deal with and make a recovery from their sexually abusive experiences. For some it was harder, and took longer, than for others. We hope this book will help you find ways of getting started on the road to recovery.

REMEMBER: You have got yourself through some really hard times in the past, so you have some important strengths. These are the strengths that are going to help you make the changes you want to make in your life.

Getting started

Surviving the crisis takes a lot of energy. But now you can begin to think about dealing with some of the feelings that we described in Section 4. It is good if you have identified someone who is going to help you and is committed to spending time with you doing this. (In this book we refer to this person as your *helper*. This could be one of the people we have talked about in Section 7, or someone else who is experienced in doing this kind of helping.)

Maybe a good place to begin is to clear up some of the confusion in your mind about the abuse. We hope that reading this book will help. You need to know as much as possible about child sexual abuse. There are other books that might be useful (check the list in Section 7). Watching TV programmes or films about sexual abuse, or talking to other victims can increase your knowledge and understanding. If you have got a helper, you might want to write out a list of questions to ask them. You deserve this information, and it can make you stronger in dealing with what has happened.

Sometimes victims are not sure exactly what happened

to them when they were abused. It may be, also, that when you told your story it was doubted or the abuser denied it or gave a totally different version. You can start to doubt yourself when this happens and may end up very confused. It is important for you to have a clear picture in your own mind so that you can stay convinced about what did happen to you. Take time to think and remember. **These are some of the things you might think about:**

- how did the abuse start?
- were there ways the abuser got you to keep it a secret?
- how long did it continue?
- what were the worst things about it?
- what did the abuser do?

This will be a painful thing to do but it will help sort out the confusion. Writing down your story is important because a lot of what has happened to you has been about keeping you confused and helpless, intentionally. Putting your story on record is a strong thing to do. Write it down and keep it safe. It is your story and no one can change that.

Tackling feelings

We have suggested two ways of getting started on reducing the confusion you may be feeling – gaining knowledge and remembering your story as clearly as possible. This will have involved some hard work for you.

But another source of confusion may be the conflicting feelings that are raging inside you. It can be difficult to tackle these and we think it is good to have help. It may not be easy for you to know what these feelings are in the first place. Some young people who have been abused cut themselves off from their feelings and bury them. Others feel overwhelmed by them. You don't have to be.

71

Recognizing, naming and understanding your feelings is a first step to reducing confusion.

It is not unusual, for example, to have both good and bad feelings towards the abuser. **Make a start at looking at these by trying to answer some questions**:

- if I am angry, what exactly am I angry about?
- if I am scared, what am I scared about?
- what good feelings do I have towards the abuser?
- do I have any good memories I want to hang on to, as well as the bad ones I want to forget?
- were/are there nice things as well as hurtful things, about him?

It is not only the abuser you will have mixed feelings about. **You may have to ask yourself similar questions about the other members of your family**:

- what are my good and bad feelings towards my parents?
- do I blame them or am I angry with them because they didn't stop the abuse?
- do I worry about either of them, and why?
- what have they done or said that was helpful/ unhelpful?
- what other feelings do I have towards other family members?

You might find it helpful to ask these questions about other adults involved in your life, or about your friends.

Now, what about you? What are your feelings about yourself? Can you begin to sort them out?

- do/did you blame yourself for the abuse?
- are you angry with yourself, and if so, why?
- do you have fears about yourself? or the way you behave?

- what are the bad feelings you have?
- what are the good ones?

REMEMBER: If you managed to stop or avoid the abuse, you can be proud you were able to do this. If you told someone, you can be proud of your courage. But it is important to remember that not many children and young people manage to do either of these and, by simply surviving the abuse, you too have reason to be proud of your strengths. If some of your behaviour has made you feel bad or ashamed, take another look at it. It was probably your way of surviving an impossible situation.

Working on feelings

Not everyone finds it easy to talk about feelings. Here are some ideas to help you if you get stuck, and things you can do with your helper:

- make a list of all sorts of feelings
- add to it by listing 'opposites', by finding 'feelings' words in stories, by identifying facial expressions in magazines, or by playing a game of drawing facial expressions and guessing each other's drawings
- check out this list when you are trying to answer the questions in this section
- rank your feelings on a scale of 1 to 10. This helps to get them into proper proportion
- recall events in your life (photos can help) and attach feelings to them
- draw yourself and other members of your family. See how you draw them. Check your feelings
- Go over Section 3 in this book and see which feelings apply to you
- Keep a pad or notebook with you so that you can note down things about your feelings – remember to keep it with you at bedtime

---

You will probably find that you have reduced some of your confusion by sorting out some of your feelings. You may also have realized that they are not as overwhelming as you thought they were. The unknown is more frightening than the known. Now you have made a start. You know more about your feelings and you know that they will often contradict each other. You know which ones you want to keep and which ones you want to work on changing. You know more about *you*.

You have a right to your feelings, whatever they are. Feelings are neither right nor wrong. But some are helpful to you and some may be causing you difficulty. Do not let anyone tell you what you 'should' or 'should not' be feeling. You may want to change some of your feelings – but that is your decision.

Letting people know

Now that you have begun to work on your feelings, you might want to let other people know and understand how you feel. Perhaps you want the abuser or family members to know. You may want to talk to friends or other victims. Although sharing feelings with other people can be helpful, it can be risky. **You might want to ask yourself:**

- will they understand what I'm talking about?
- will they care?
- can I trust them?
- will they use what I tell them against me sometime?
- what will they think of me?

We have said before that we don't think it is possible to deal with all that has happened to you without help. Talking with an adult helper is a good way of deciding what you want to share, how you want to share it and who you want to share it with.

Sometimes it is useful to rehearse. One of the ways you can do this is to imagine that the person you want to talk to is sitting in an empty chair in the room. Try to talk directly to it. At first this may feel a bit strange, but if you can get used to it, it can be helpful. Or you can ask an adult helper to play the part of the person. Writing down what you want to say is sometimes useful in anticipating how the person will take it.

The right to rage

Anger is a natural response to being abused. Yet sometimes this is the hardest feeling to express. We are all taught that being angry is bad and unacceptable, and that controlling anger is good. For some, anger is a terrifying emotion associated with people being violent and out of control. You might feel, for some of these reasons, that you can't express anger unless you feel very safe, either on your own or with somebody who gives you permission and makes it okay.

The chances are that you were probably not able to feel, express or act on your rage when you were being abused. Rather than be angry with the person who abused you, you probably denied or twisted your anger. Remember the abuser was in control – he was in the position to threaten, cajole or persuade you into seeing it his way and to effectively stifle or deflect your anger. And it is pretty certain that, as a result, you turned your anger inwards against yourself. You may have wanted to hurt or kill yourself. You may have felt yourself to be bad, criticized yourself unrelentingly, devalued yourself. Or you may have smothered your anger with food, deadened it with alcohol or stifled it with solvent abuse. Anger kept inside you may have made you ill or depressed.

Having been taught to blame yourself, you stay angry with the small child that is inside you – the child who was vulnerable, who was hurt, who couldn't protect itself, who needed affection, who experienced physical sensations it could make no sense of. But this child did nothing wrong. This child doesn't deserve your anger.

You may also have turned your anger on people other than the abuser – sometimes with some justification, but often with none. If you haven't got into physical fights, you may have picked verbal battles or looked for things to criticize. (We have found that sometimes boys are more likely to divert their anger like this, and some can also be sexually abusive themselves towards other children or young people.) Or you may have found yourself in raging tempers at nothing at all. Usually that means that *you* get the blame, that *you* get the label.

It is time that you directed your anger where it really belongs – at the person who abused you and took advantage of your helplessness. This is *your right* – don't be afraid of it.

Getting in touch

The first step is recognizing your anger and allowing yourself to feel it:

- who are you angry with? the abuser? a parent? yourself? the world?
- are you just annoyed or are you furious?

Look at what you normally do with angry feelings:

- do you keep them bottled up?
- do you tell people about them?
- do you do something to change what is making you angry, or do you remain passive?
- do you yell at people?
- do you tease and criticize?
- do you lash out?
- do you break things?
- do you hurt yourself?
- what have you done to express your anger in the past?

- what would you like to do to show people that you are angry?
- do you ever secretly think about the things you would like to do to show your anger?

Here are some ways that have helped other people get their angry feelings about abuse out in the open. You might feel inhibited at first when you are trying them – but they often do work:

- Imagine a child you know or care about being treated in the same way you were treated.
- Read other victims' stories. (There are some in Section 3.) You can perhaps feel angry for them.
- Go somewhere safe and get into an angry posture – make angry faces, shout and swear, scream. Get a friend to scream with you!
- Try asking your helper to sit in front of you and put up their hands with the palms facing you. Now push against them with your palms. Push hard. Get your helper to push back. Get mad.
- Punch cushions. Hit the bed with a tennis racquet. A rolled-up newspaper is just as good – and makes a great noise.
- With your helper, act out situations which make you feel angry. Make some rules about this – no hurting anyone, no hurting yourself.

Sometimes giving vent to your anger can make you aware of other kinds of feelings as a powerful aftermath – loneliness, sadness and grief. It is a good idea to have someone around who understands what you are trying to do, and can comfort you.

Here are some ideas for directly targeting your anger:

- Draw pictures of the abuser. Tell them what you would like to do to them. Tear them up into little pieces. Put them on the wall and throw things at them.

- Make your own models of the abuser in clay or plasticine. Stick pins in them. Squash them. Break them into little pieces.
- Imagine the abuser in 'the empty chair'. If you can't say angry things to him, get your helper to do it.
- Listen to family members, friends or your helper being angry on your behalf.
- Make a list of the ways in which the abuse has affected you. You are bound to find things to be angry about.
- Write a letter to the person who abused you (even if the person is no longer around and even if he is dead). You shouldn't send the letter. It is private – just for you. Write all your angry thoughts in it. Don't hold back. Call them all the names you want. Tell them how hurt you are and why.
- Try dictating the letter on to a tape-recorder.
- Re-read your letter, or play back your tape. Add some more before you put it somewhere safe.
- Or take out your letter and rip it to shreds. Tear it into the smallest pieces possible.
- If you are angry with other people, do the same for them.

Sometimes you can feel so much anger that it is hard to talk without losing control. Try some physical exercise. Run, jog, take the dog for a walk. Try some aerobics. Jump up and down.

At some point or another you may have strong feelings of wanting to get back at the person who has hurt you. You dream of revenge – or even murder. Wanting revenge is a natural impulse, a sane response. Of course you can't act on it. But let yourself imagine it to your heart's content. That is one way of getting it out of your system.

REMEMBER: Being angry with someone doesn't cancel out the good feelings you might have about them. You have a right to your anger. Expressing it clears the way for you to feel whole again.

Dealing with fears

Victims of sexual abuse have much to fear. Some of these fears can be real and immediate – like the fear that the abuse will happen again, or once the abuse has come to light, that the abuser or others will get back at them. No child or young person should be left unprotected in such a situation and adults have a duty to act so that you can be reassured of safety.

But you may be afraid of so many things that you are in a constant state of fear, without really knowing what it is in particular that is making you feel like this. It helps to name your fears. Naming things gives them less of a hold. **It can be helpful to list your fears and think of**:

- what you have feared in the past
- what you are now fearful of
- what triggers off fears
- what are your greatest fears
- which fears are realistic and which are not
- what you or others can do to reduce these fears

Go over these with your helper. Some people think that the more you talk about them and relive them, the less they control your life.

Some fears can be tackled relatively straightforwardly. For example, a common fear that victims have is that they will have suffered permanent physical damage. In fact, this is rarely the case. But if this is a fear that you have, you should see a doctor to have this checked.

Other fears are more complicated to deal with. Many children who have been abused are afraid to trust or love again because their love and trust have been betrayed by the abuser. They may also have felt badly let down by others. If this is how you are feeling, it may take quite a bit of time before you are able to love and trust again. Give yourself that time – and if you feel that by not trusting them you are hurting someone you like, try explaining that to them.

79

Many victims tell us that they have difficulties about sleeping. Their fears and anxieties seem to get exaggerated at night. They often have difficulty getting to sleep and many report recurring and distressing nightmares. Some dread their dreams so much that they are afraid to go to sleep.

Here we make some suggestions to cope with this – many of these have come from the victims themselves.

Things that can help

- Have a safety ritual – this can include checking doors, windows, cupboards and so on. Don't be embarrassed about this.
- Try to have a relaxing time just before bed – a hot bath, a warm drink, some soothing music (avoid horror movies).
- Keep a night-light on.
- It is great if you can have someone to talk to, who will waken you properly from the nightmare.
- Some victims have nightmares and waken up in a state of panic or terror at about the same time every night. If you have this particular problem, and you have someone willing to help, try asking them to waken you, for 10 mins or so, shortly *before* your usual waking time. If you can keep this up over a period of 2–3 weeks, it can sometimes break the pattern.
- Listen to music on a personal stereo or radio (you may identify a particular piece of music that helps) or watch TV when you waken from the nightmare.
- If you wake 'frozen' with anxiety from a bad dream, it is sometimes frightening to break the silence with sudden noise from a radio or TV. One survivor has told us that she starts by talking quietly to herself or sings a song. She finds this reassuring.
- Keep a cuddly toy – remember you are never too old for this.
- Practise with your helper bringing into your mind (visualizing) a pleasant scene which you can use to blot out the images left over from your nightmare.

- If you like animals, see if it is possible to have your pet in the room. One boy has told us how much it helped to have his dog in his room at night.
- Keep the good book you are reading by your bedside.
- Find out about 'relaxation'. Maybe your helper could make a relaxation tape for you to play when you are panicky.
- There are good simple breathing exercises that help control panic and anxiety:
  Try counting breaths.
  Make your 'out' breath much longer than your 'in' breath.
  Lie with one hand on your chest and one hand on your stomach. Try to breathe so that the hand on your stomach rises higher than the one on your chest. This makes your breathing deeper and slower.

Take your fears, and your ways of coping with them, seriously. Even if some of these ways seem silly and you want to give them up, don't do this all at once. Some people's fears go beyond the actual abuse and become associated with certain kinds of people, certain surroundings, sights, sounds, and smells. Anxiety like this can make you feel powerless and slow down your recovery.

More things that can help

- Make a list of 'reminders of the abuse' or all the situations when you get scared.
- Go over this list with your helper.
- Work out some ways of dealing with these situations.
- Talk about them some more – just recognizing them might help reduce anxiety.
- Act out some of these situations with your helper, and find ways of trying out alternative feelings and reactions.
- Find out about self-defence classes in your area. We are not suggesting that you should be able to defend yourself, but young people have said that these classes

81

help them to be more assertive and confident. So can martial arts – Karate Tai Chi, Kendo – or dancing, drama and physical sports.

- Remember the breathing exercises – you can do them anywhere, at any time.

Your 'alert list'

If your abuse was in the past, then one of your fears may be that you will be abused by someone else in the future because you have not been able to 'spot' an abusive situation. The following list has been drawn up by survivors of sexual abuse. They suggest that you should be alert if an adult or older person is:

- treating you differently from others
- wanting to spend time alone with you, making excuses to go places with you or having others leave
- accidently-on-purpose touching your private parts or brushing against your breasts while wrestling, rubbing his body against yours
- looking at or touching your body and saying it is an inspection or that he wants to see how you are developing
- putting lotion or ointment on when your mother or others are not around or when nothing is wrong
- accidently-on-purpose coming in your room while you are undressed or when you are in the bathroom
- not respecting your privacy, coming into your room without knocking and not allowing you to close doors to your bedroom or bathroom
- asking questions or making accusations about sexual activity between you and your boyfriends
- teaching sex education by showing you pornographic pictures, or by showing his body or touching yours
- saying sexual things about your body or how you dress
- talking to you about sexual things he has done
- telling you private things about his wife/your mother

- saying you are special, different, the only one who really understands, better than his wife, or adult partner
- treating you like an adult/him acting like a kid
- giving you special privileges or favours and making you feel you owe him something in return
- treating you worse than others
- not letting you have friends
- telling you not to tell your mother or other people about things that happen between you
- coming into your bedroom at night
- accidently-on-purpose letting his dressing gown come apart, or letting you see him walking around without clothes on
- doing anything that makes you feel uncomfortable or embarrassed in a way you can't explain

Getting rid of the guilt

Almost all victims feel guilty about what has happened to them. You will almost certainly feel that you were in some way to blame or that you were responsible for the abuse.

Let us remind you that abusers are *always* totally responsible for sexual abuse. There was nothing you did or said that caused it to happen, and very little within your power that could have stopped it. We hope that if you have talked to anyone about being abused they also will have pointed this out. Nevertheless, we recognize that even hearing this said, or reading it, will not necessarily stop you *feeling* guilty. It is this feeling that can stop you from getting on with your life in a positive way. Getting rid of guilt is central to recovery, but it is one of the hardest things to do. Guilt feelings have a habit of returning just when you think you have laid them to rest. Each time they do, you have to work through them again.

Once again, it is important to be clear about what your

feelings are. Make up a 'Guilt List'. **Do you feel guilty because**:

- it was something about you that 'invited' the abuse?
- you were the kind of child who 'deserved' it?
- you enjoyed the special attention involved . . . or the rewards . . . or you took money?
- you 'used' the secret to get some kind of advantage over the abuser?
- you experienced pleasurable physical feelings associated with the abuse?
- you didn't tell?
- you didn't do enough to stop the abuse?
- you didn't do enough to prevent brothers and sisters being abused?
- by telling, you have upset your family or brought them unwelcome attention?
- you are responsible for breaking up the family?
- you have brought punishment on the abuser?
- you have had angry feelings towards family or friends who have not helped you?
- you have behaved in destructive or self-destructive ways?

We have been told by many victims that these are the things that are on their Guilt Lists. You might have some of them on yours. Or you might have others of your own. But *feeling* guilty about these does not mean that you *are* guilty. Look at your list again. Can you decide which of these 'guilts' are realistic and which are not? While you are doing this, be prepared to argue with yourself. **These are some things to remember:**

- There are a variety of ways that abusers engage children in sexual activity. There are also many ways, both subtle and unsubtle, that they ensure secrecy. Sometimes it can take time before a child understands what is going on and that it is wrong

- Every child needs affection. Every child needs attention. If these are not offered in healthy, non-sexual ways children will take them in whatever ways they can
- When we are touched sexually, we can't always stop our bodies from responding. Our whole physiology is designed to give us pleasure. These are natural bodily responses and we do not always have control over them
- Some kinds of behaviour may seem very destructive, but when examined more closely may be viewed as a cry for help, or a way of surviving an impossible situation, or a way of cutting off from pain and confusion

Have you argued with yourself? Has this helped you to reduce your 'Guilt List'? You might have to come back to this from time to time, and go over it with your helper.

You might have found that some of your behaviour has given you what you think are justified guilt feelings. This is the behaviour you might want to start changing. The next section of the book might help.

Here are some other ways that victims have found helpful in getting rid of guilt:

- talking to other victims (if possible in a group)
- putting forward arguments to persuade other victims they were not to blame
- making up posters or slogans that would help remind them and other victims that they were not to blame

For those of you who were abused at a young age:

- Try to identify a child you know and care about who is now the same age as you were when the abuse started. Ask yourself if they would be to blame if they were abused. Ask yourself if they could do anything to stop it.

- Draw a picture, or find a photograph of yourself at the age you were when the abuse was going on. Ask yourself what this small child could have done?
- Argue with the little child in the picture. Tell them they were not to blame. Write them a letter explaining why.

I'm 'different'?

Many people who are victims of child sexual abuse feel dirty or shameful as a result. So they feel 'different' from other people. You will recognize some of the worries victims have expressed to us: 'People can tell by looking at me what has happened . . . I can't go down the street without feeling that people will know . . .'

It can help to know that you are not so different. Many other people have had similar experiences. Remind yourself of what you have learned about the statistics of sexual abuse. Think about what they really mean. Next time you are in a crowd – in school, on a bus, in the cinema – look around you. Some of the people around you were probably victims too. You can't tell by looking, can you? No one can identify victims of sexual abuse by looking at them. If you could it would be a lot easier to stop the abuse of children.

Still, you may *feel* different. You may believe that if people knew about the abuse, they would not like you. And this just might be true of some people. Some may be ignorant about sexual abuse, and may wrongly think it was your fault. Some may be afraid of abuse happening to them and be unable to face their own fears. Some people may think that because you have been sexually abused, you know a lot about sex, perhaps 'more than you should'. They may think you 'strange' or different for that reason. So really it is about *them*, not about *you*.

But people are learning more about sexual abuse and are more likely to know that you, as the victim, suffered

86

from what the abuser did. They will realize the courage you needed to survive. They will like you, or dislike you because of the person you are and the way you behave, not because of what has happened to you.

REMEMBER: You do not need to feel ashamed of being a victim. There is nothing wrong or bad about you because of it.

I can't take it any more

Sometimes you may feel so bad you want to die. The pain is so great, you hate yourself so much, and you are so afraid and lonely that you really don't want to live. You might get preoccupied with images and thoughts of death and dying. It's important that you are able to talk to someone about these feelings, but it is *essential* not to act on them. It's understandable to feel as devastated as you feel. It is just not okay to hurt yourself.

Already far too many young people have not had proper support and, out of despair, have hurt or killed themselves. This can't go on. We are not going to lose you. You deserve to live.

Read again what we have said about anger. When you feel so bad that you want to die, there is an anger inside you that needs to be let loose on the person or people who hurt you.

This is a critical time for you. Get help. If the first help isn't helpful, get other help. Don't give up. Talk to someone, a teacher, a relative, for example. Use a phoneline. (Check the numbers in Section 7.) Contact your helper.

When you feel bad enough to want to die, it is hard to imagine that you could ever feel any other way. But you can. And will. The feelings will pass. Hang on. Each time you get through a bad time like this, you are learning to reach out for help, and building up your strength. And you have demonstrated to the abuser that he can't destroy you.

Tackling it together

If you get a chance to join a group with others who have had similar experiences to yourself, you might find this really helpful. Teenagers have told us that joining a group was a completely different experience from other kinds of help. They felt that the group became a really important part of their recovery.

The girls in one group we know felt so strongly about it that, when they knew we were writing this book, they wanted to say something about the experience of being in a group.

They talk about the group breaking down the isolation and loneliness that surrounds abuse . . .

'The group has helped me to see I'm not the only person in the world who has been sexually abused.'

'Before I came to the group I was sometimes screaming inside because I wanted to tell somebody. I think it's better in the group because people share these bad secrets.'

'Before, I used to sit and cry about any worries I had or about something that was bothering me, but now I know I have people I can talk to and get everything out.'

. . . and they feel that they are among people who, because they have had similar experiences, can really understand what they are going through . . .

'The people in the group . . . have got a lot of feelings like you.'

'It helps you when you listen to other people's problems and you have got one the same.'

'Talking to people and having people around who know and understand how you feel . . . .'

The group feels safe and they can trust each other . . .

'I'm not so frightened any more.'

'In the group, I feel comfortable and safe.'

'Now I know I can talk and nobody knows except us.'

'Since I have been in the group, I've been able to speak more openly.'

'I've told the group things that I would never tell anyone else.'

. . . and they can get both practical advice and support from each other . . .

'If you feel upset or if you have a problem, the rest of the group give you advice about what to do.'

'If you feel down, you come to the group . . . and just being there makes you feel good again.'

Finally, they talk about hope. Seeing others starting to feel stronger gives them hope that they too can be strong again. The group worked really well for these girls. Maybe it could work for you?

Face to face

Meeting the abuser face to face is often an issue with victims. Some people are very scared of being in a situation where they might meet the abuser. But there are times when victims feel they want to confront their abusers for various reasons. Maybe they want to hear him admitting to what he has done, and that he is sorry. They want him to hear how badly they have been hurt, or how angry they are with him. They might want revenge. Or they want to hear him say they were right to tell and that he still loves them.

Are you worried about meeting the abuser (perhaps accidentally) or being in his presence? If you have a helper or a group, rehearse ways of dealing with this –

things you can say or do to keep yourself from panicking and to keep yourself safe. Look over the section in this book on dealing with fears.

If you want to confront your abuser, it is important that *you don't do this on your own*. Remember that you could be in a very vulnerable position. You need somebody with you and you need to prepare what you want to say. (Preferably discuss this thoroughly with your helper.) Prepare yourself for not necessarily hearing the things you want to hear. Abusers don't change overnight.

Forgive and forget?

We have talked about this process as a 'Road to Recovery'. Some people might tell you that the final destination is forgiveness. We do not feel that you should necessarily see this as your goal. Why should you forgive? Your abuser has stolen from you – he has no right to expect forgiveness too. You have given enough.

But if you do find yourself feeling some compassion for your abuser or for family members you have been very angry with, let it happen. Often, it will be because you are starting to feel stronger and beginning to like yourself a bit more.

Eventually there *is* a need for you to make peace with your past and move on, but whether or not this resolution involves forgiveness is a personal matter. You may never feel forgiveness and that's perfectly okay.

Section 6

Making Changes

'I believe not only in my ability to survive, but to flourish.'

Lyn Swenson, in *I Never Told Anyone*, an anthology of writings by women survivors

Moving On

In the last section we tried to suggest ways in which you could help yourself to get through the specific effects of sexual abuse, and we looked at the ways you could deal with the feelings surrounding it. Now we want to look at you as a person, at how you want to be and what you want to become. We want to take a more long-term view. We want to consider not only how you are going to 'survive' – but also at how you are going to 'flourish'. You might want to look at how you act and how you think about yourself. We all should do this sometimes. Does some of your behaviour cause you problems, cut you off from people, or even cause people to react badly to you? Are there some changes you would like to make?

You may well be thinking that it is not possible for you to change – that this is 'just me, that's the way I am'. Making changes of any kind is hard work. It usually seems easier to stay the way you have always been. When you make a change, especially in an important area in your life, such as how you act with friends, you take risks. For example, it may feel safer to stay home and not go to a party than to go and feel nervous about making conversation. Or it might be easier to be quiet and keep your feelings to yourself rather than risk being made fun of. Or it might be less frightening to stick to your 'I don't care' act when you are hurt, rather than give in to tears and let people know how you really feel.

It is important to recognize that until now you have had good reason for not changing – you have been protecting yourself. You have been expecting others to dislike you, disappoint you or hurt you. As a helpless child you may have waited in vain for someone to rescue you, so as a young person you still may be looking for solutions outside of yourself.

In looking to the future you now need to look at how you can become responsible for yourself, and for your relationships with other people. It will take time and perseverance to change negative ways of thinking and replace them with more positive ones. You might get discouraged and wonder if it is worth the effort. If you can keep trying, we think you will be a happier person and that is what you deserve.

I'm worthless?

'I don't deserve anything . . . Nobody could possibly like me . . . Whatever I do, I'm never going to be acceptable . . . Nobody could ever really love me . . . What I want doesn't count.'

It is easy to see how someone who has been abused, particularly over a period of time, can see themselves like this. But you are never going to be able to believe that anyone can care about you unless you have *learned to love yourself*. Maybe this is a concept you have never really thought about before. Well, consider it now. How can you open yourself up to the idea of being important, worthwhile or loveable, if you still don't love yourself a little. Everyone needs to do this.

You can start by looking after yourself, by taking care of yourself. Tell yourself you are worth looking after. Learn to hear people when they tell you about your good qualities. Listen to compliments – even though you are tempted to contradict and deny them. Look at ways of getting yourself into shape and getting healthy and fit. How you look and dress are often important reflections of how you feel. If you have been neglecting this, how about spending some time on yourself.

Think of things you *like* doing (that are not harmful to you) and work on the possibility of *doing* them. Tell yourself you deserve it – because you do. You have had pain in your life, but you may not know much about pleasure. Maybe you will have to learn what's fun for you and what you enjoy. Give yourself permission to do this. Allow yourself to do 'childish' things – you may have missed out on some of those pleasures.

No matter what our experiences have been, we all

have our good and bad qualities. We would be willing to bet that you have spent a lot of time dwelling on your bad ones. Hopefully, in learning to care for yourself and, in the process, loving yourself a little, you will be able to believe in some of the good qualities which you most certainly have.

Most of us find it quite hard to say what we are good at. It might be a good idea to get your helper to draw up a list with you of your good qualities, your strong points, the things about yourself that you like and what you are good at. That list will be longer than you think.

Saying no

Another way of looking after yourself and feeling good is to be able to set limits: learning how *not* to do things just to please other people without regard to yourself; learning to sometimes say 'no'. By setting your own limits, you are protecting yourself and learning to have some freedom of choice.

There are lots of different kinds of situations in which you might want to say no. Start with the easy ones. If you've hardly ever said no, your first attempts may feel awkward or even rude. You might want to make long explanations as soon as you've said it.

Saying no doesn't have to be loud or hostile (although it can be if you want it to). As you get better at it, you'll be able to do so with a simple statement: 'No, I don't want to; No thanks; No, I'd rather not; No, I can't do that.'

As you start saying no to other people, you are learning to say yes to yourself. You are listening to your own needs and are able to put yourself first some of the time. You also need to find ways of saying what you want or feel, to ask for things in ways that people can respond to in a positive way. That might mean looking at some of the ways you've done this before. If you've been clingy, loud and aggressive or simply been quiet but resentful, you might want to make changes.

Taking care of yourself

Some victims turn to alcohol, drugs or solvents in order to escape, to find relief or to feel better. Trying to meet your needs in this way can put you at risk of becoming addicted. And addictions can destroy your body, cut you off from your feelings, make you feel worse about yourself and sometimes kill you. Remember, addiction can be both a survival tool and a self-destructive habit. Solvents, alcohol and drugs are effective short-term ways to numb feelings, suppress memories and escape from pain. But to make a recovery from your abuse, you need to *experience* your feelings and look clearly at your life. If you think you have an addiction problem – or are worried that you could become addicted – try to be honest with yourself. Then try to be honest with someone who will help you to get the specialist help you will definitely need.

There are eating disorders that can be used in similar ways but can also, in their turn, present you with problems. The life-threatening conditions of anorexia (obsessively controlling food intake to tiny amounts) and bulimia (a pattern of bingeing and vomiting) are common in a society that admires thinness and despises fat. Girls, in particular are susceptible to these messages, and sexual abuse can make the problem worse.

Some people falsely believe that if they don't grow breasts, develop full hips, become curvy, they won't be attractive and no one will force them into being sexual. For others, not eating is an attempt to exert control. By strictly controlling what they do and don't take into their body, they are trying unconsciously, perhaps, to regain the power that was taken from them as children. And for others, anorexia is a way of saying no to a life that has given them abuse, pain, fear and humiliation. They are not instantly killing themselves, but eating only enough not to die. And sometimes they do die. Bulimia is closely related in its motivations and is just as dangerous.

Again we would like to emphasize that, if you think

this is, or is becoming, a problem for you, *get specialist help*. We are aware that one of the features of this condition is that the person is often reluctant to recognize the problem. So we are anxious to add that, if someone in your life is suggesting to you that you need help with this, try to listen to them.

Staying in the world

Some children/young people who are abused have learned to 'turn off' body pain and sensations. They 'go into a trance' to cut themselves off and protect themselves from pain and confusion. Others escape by 'pretending to sleep', or by creating a fantasy world they can almost permanently inhabit. Some split themselves into two different personalities – one to deal with the abuse situation and one to exist in the world outside. Some of this might be familiar to you.

The problem with being emotionally or physically disconnected is that as well as cutting yourself off from the painful feelings, you also cut yourself off from the positive ones. If you are only half in the world, you are missing out on so much of its richness. Although fantasy can provide us all with a source of creativity, if you live too permanently in the fantasy world that is your haven, it can become your prison.

You might not be able to decide to what extent this is a major problem for you, but make a start by discussing it with your helper.

Ways of relating

'Back off . . . keep your distance . . . I don't trust you.'
'If I say what I really want, I won't get it.'
'Here I am, walk all over me.'
'I'm tough, nothing hurts me . . . I don't care . . . what difference does it make.'
'I'm a walking time-bomb – watch out.'
'I'm ill, look after me.'

'If I serve people and am dutiful, I'll please them.'
'I'm hurt, so I'll hide.'
'You sort it out for me.'

We all give out messages about ourselves, and we all interpret messages we get from others. Sometimes we misread them.

You, as a victim, have had your trust abused, and this makes it particularly difficult to open yourself to people and trust them. Some of the quotes above might be familiar to you as ways that you have hidden or defended yourself from other people.

Sometimes it takes a very long time to allow yourself to trust others again. And when you can't trust, a vicious cycle begins. The less you trust, the less likely you are to have friends or have people who are going to help you. The more isolated you become, the less you *can* trust others. When you can't seem to make friends, you may think that there is something wrong with you. So you feel more vulnerable and will tend to guard yourself rather than trust enough to be open.

Trusting someone is always risky. Sometimes the trust you place in another person will be rewarded, other times you will be let down. You will know how painful it is to trust someone and then be hurt. Do you find yourself suspicious of the motives of everyone? Are there some people that you allow yourself to trust, at least a little? Is there anyone you have trusted who hasn't let you down? Is there anyone you trust right now?

Going through life without trusting anyone would be very lonely for you. We would like to think that the more you allow yourself to trust somebody and find them reliable, the more willing you will be to trust other people in the future. Don't feel you have to take it too quickly. Take time to consider the person you want to trust. But don't give up.

Getting along with others

We appreciate how difficult it might be for victims of sexual abuse to know how to get along well with people their own age. You may have had little chance to be with others while growing up. You might not feel that you share the same interests as schoolmates – especially if you have had to take on a lot of responsibility around the house. You might have acted older than your age, or you might have avoided people because you felt 'different'.

There are lots of reasons why you might feel uncomfortable, awkward and nervous about making friends or being with people. Learning to get along easily with others is just like any other skill. It takes practice. You get better at it gradually but it takes a conscious effort and it is hard to take the knock-backs you might get. Try things out a day at a time. And praise yourself for trying. It might help to remind yourself that the people you want to approach may well have some of the same difficulties, even if it's for different reasons.

Sex . . . and love?

People sometimes tend to assume that young people who have been sexually abused know all about sex and even 'more than they should'. We know from working with victims that this is far from the truth, in fact it is often quite the opposite. We have said before that not having knowledge and information can make you feel powerless, so we feel it is important that you find out all you can about your body, and how it works sexually. There are a number of books available in libraries and bookshops and we suggest some at the end of this book.

Having factual knowledge is not necessarily enough. Most young people are not sure about sex and are given very confused messages about it in our society. But victims of sexual abuse have particular problems. They have, after all, been introduced to sex in a totally inappropriate way. They may think of sex as dirty, shameful, fearful and to be avoided for ever. On the other hand they may feel that sex is the only way they know how to act, how to please and get acceptance. For some, it has been the only way to get 'love'. This puts them at risk of further abuse because potential abusers exploit their confusion and their need for love and acceptance. For some, particularly boys, it distorts their attitudes so much that they become sexually abusive towards others younger and weaker than themselves. (If you feel that this is in any way a problem for you, it is *essential* that you get some professional help.)

Sex itself is not wrong. It was the way you were involved in sex that was wrong. Sex can give you pleasure and happiness. Sex within a loving, caring relationship can be great. It usually takes time for this kind of relationship to develop, so go slowly. Don't jump into a sexual relationship. And if you decide that sex is not for you at present, that's okay. You can have warm, close relationships without sex.

To help you decide how you are going to deal with your own sexuality, as well as with the sexual overtures from other people, we would once again recommend *Too Close Encounters – And What To Do About Them* (see Section 7).

Coming to terms

We talked earlier in the book about how recovery is not necessarily about forgiveness. But for you we hope there will be, sooner or later, some resolution. And this will mean coming to terms with what has happened. For some of you this will be a continuing process that you may have to return to at various times in your life.

For those of you who were abused by someone in the family, or who did not get the support of your parent/s, you will have missed the safe, consistent loving experience every child deserves. But you can't rewrite the past. You must say goodbye to the 'wish' for the perfect parents and continue with the rest of your life. When you give up the longing for what might have been, you make room for what can be, and for the 'real' people in your life – even if they are not perfect.

Victim to survivor

Throughout this book we have referred to people who have been sexually abused as 'victims'. This is because, in our contact with children and young people who have had this experience, we have learned the many ways in which they can be hurt. We have sometimes been overwhelmed by admiration for their courage, and our hearts have gone out to them in their struggle to move on. We have also been very moved by their spirit of survival. We know that with some help, *you* will be proud to join the many people who have fought through and have been able 'not only to survive, but to flourish'.

Section 7

Information and Resources

Who are the helpers?

These are some of the professional people who work with children and young people. Any of them could give you special help – but some are more likely to play this role than others. At different stages you might find some kinds of help more appropriate than others. The list doesn't include *all* the people who might be helpers.

social worker	**youth worker**	**health visitor**
psychologist	**school nurse**	**care worker**
foster parent	**teacher**	**child psychiatrist**

There are voluntary agencies who can be involved with young people and who sometimes offer specific resources for victims of sexual abuse. These include:

Royal Scottish Society for the Prevention of Cruelty to Children
National Society for the Prevention of Cruelty to Children
Rape Crisis
Action Against Incest
Phonelines (national and local)

All of these agencies offer counselling of different kinds. Apart from RSSPCC and NSPCC, they would not necessarily report sexual abuse to a social worker.

Of course, for some of you, a lot of the helping can come from your immediate friends or family.

What the words mean

In the process of telling and getting help, you may well have to give an account of what happened to you. We have come across young people who have been asked questions about sexual activity that included words and phrases that they did not understand. This was often because these words were the 'correct' terms and not the ones in everyday language. We thought it would be useful to record some of the most common of these:

The sexual organs can be referred to as **genitals**. A man or a boy has a **penis** and **testicles**; a girl or a woman has a **vagina** and a **clitoris**.

When sexually aroused, a penis becomes enlarged (**erection**). Rubbing or stimulating the sexual organs is referred to as **masturbation**. When the penis continues to be stimulated to a certain point (**climax**) a white fluid (**semen**) comes out (an **ejaculation**). When female sexual organs are stimulated, the climax is called an **orgasm**. **Oral sex** describes any activity that uses the mouth to stimulate the sexual organs. The **anus** is the back passage and **anal sex** refers to activity involving this.

Other books to read

About Bodies, Sex and Sexuality

Jane Cousins, *Make It Happy*, Penguin, 1980

Helen Benedict, *Safe, Strong and Streetwise: The Teenage Survival Guide*, Hodder and Stoughton, 1988

Peter Mayle, *What's Happening to Me?*, Macmillan, 1978

Peter Mayle, *Where Do I Come From?*, Macmillan, 1978

Adrina E. McCormack and Elizabeth McCall Smith, *All About Sex*, W & R Chambers, 1987

Kathy McCoy and Dr Charles Wibbelsman, *The Teenage Body Book*, Piatkus, 1989

Susan Meredith, *Understanding the Facts of Life*, Usborne, 1985

Rosemary Stones, *Too Close Encounters – and What to do About Them*, Magnet, 1987

About Sexual Abuse

Ellen Bass and Laura Davis, *The Courage to Heal: A Guide for Women Survivors of Child Sexual Abuse*, Harper and Row, 1988

Ellen Bass and Louise Thornton, *I Never Told Anyone: Writings by Women Survivors of Child Sexual Abuse*, Harper and Row, 1983

Lyn Daugherty, *Why Me*, Mother Courage Press, USA, 1984

Michele Elliot, *Keeping Safe: A Practical Guide to Talking with Children*, Bedford Square Press, 1985

Liz Hall and Siobhan Lloyd, *Surviving Child Sexual Abuse*, The Falmer Press, 1989

Sarah Nelson, *Incest, Fact and Myth*, Stramullion Press, 1985

Khadj Rouf, *Secrets* (two versions – one dealing with white families, one dealing with black). Available from the Children's Society, Purnell Distribution Centre, Paulton, Bristol BS18 5LQ

Oralee Wachter, *No More Secrets For Me*, Puffin, 1986

First Person Accounts
Maya Angelou, *I Know Why the Caged Bird Sings*, Virago, 1984

Sylvia Fraser, *My Father's House*, Virago, 1989

Eleanore Hill, *The Family Secret*, Laurel, 1985

Jacqueline Spring, *Cry Hard and Swim*, Virago, 1987

Novels
Lyn Morgan, *Megan's Secret*, Papers Inc., New Zealand, 1987 (Written particularly for teenagers)

Alice Walker, *The Color Purple*, The Women's Press, 1983

Some of these books are published in other countries and can be hard to get. If you have any difficulties, most can be obtained from Bookstall Services, 86 Abbey Street, Derby. Tel: Derby 368039

Useful Phone Lines

In Britain

Childline
Freepost 111
London EC4 4BB   **Tel: 0800 1111**

The phone number is the same wherever you live; the service is free and open 24 hours. This phone line is so busy that it is sometimes difficult to get through, so keep trying.

National Children's Home
Family Network   **Tel: 071 226 2033**

There are local phone numbers – the national number will give them where they exist. This phone line, like Childline, deals with a range of problems and can give you phone numbers that will help with specific problems.

The National Society for the Prevention
of Cruelty to Children (NSPCC)
67, Saffron Hill
London EC1N 8RS   **Tel: 071 242 1626**

Local numbers in the telephone directory.

Royal Scottish Society for the Prevention
of Cruelty to Children
Melville House
41, Polworth Terrace
Edinburgh EH11 1NU   **Tel: 031 337 8539/8530**

Local numbers in the telephone directory.

London Rape Crisis   Tel: 071 837 1600
Glasgow Rape Crisis   Tel: 041 221 8448

Rape Crisis Centres are listed in the local telephone directory. They will be able to provide contact numbers for 'Action Against Incest' groups where they exist.

British Pregnancy Advisory Service
7, Belgrave Road
London SW1V 1QB   Tel: 071 222 0985

Brook Advisory Centres
153a, East St
London SE17 2SD   Tel: 071 708 1234

Family Planning Association
27, Mortimer St
London W1N 7RJ   Tel: 071 636 7866

All three agencies offer advice on pregnancy and contraception. For local phone numbers, see your telephone directory.

Samaritans

Local numbers in the telephone directory. Counselling for those in despair. You can ask the operator to put you through. This is a 24 hour service.

In Canada

Kids Help Phoneline (national)   1 800 668 6868
(**Jennesse J'écoute in Quebec**)

In **Edmonton**, **Calgary**, **Vancouver** and **Victoria**, call
Operator '0' ask for Zenith 1234

Halifax Sexual Assault Line	902 425 0122
Montreal Sexual Assault Line	514 934 4504
Toronto Rape Crisis	416 964 8080
Ottawa Sexual Assault Support Centre	613 234 2266
Ottawa Child Abuse Line	613 737 1700
Thunder Bay Physical & Sexual Assault Crisis Centre	807 344 4502
Winnipeg Child & Family Service Agencies Emergency Line	204 944 4050
Winnipeg Sexual Assault Line	204 786 8631
Regina Child Protection Services	306 787 3760
Regina Sexual Assault Line	306 352 0434
Saskatoon Child Protection Services	306 933 6077
Saskatoon Sexual Assault	306 244 2224
Edmonton Sexual Assault Line	403 423 4121
Calgary Sexual Assault Line	403 244 1353
Vancouver Rape Crisis	604 875 6011
Victoria Sexual Assault Centre	604 383 3232

(local numbers usually on first page of telephone
directory)

Planned Parenthood Federation of Canada,
1 Nicholas Street, Suite 430,
Ottawa, Ontario.
K1N 7B7   Tel: 613 238 4474

Planned Parenthood of Toronto,
36 B Prince Arthur Avenue,
Toronto, Ontario.
M5R 1A9   Tel: 416 961 0113

Facts of Life Line   Tel: 416 961 3200
(local numbers in telephone directory)

Association of Children's Aid Societies,
1027 McNichol Avenue East, 2nd Floor,
Scarborough, Ontario.
M1W 3W6   Tel: 416 491 1664

Children's Aid Society of Metropolitan Toronto,
32 Charles Street East,
Toronto, Ontario.
M4Y 1R9   Tel: 416 924 4646
(local numbers in telephone director)

Canadian Child Welfare Association,
2211 Promenade Riverside Drive, Suite 401,
Ottawa, Ontario.
K1H 7X5   Tel: 613 738 0697

Institute for the Prevention of Child Abuse,
25 Spadina Road,
Toronto, Ontario.
M5R 2S9   Tel: 416 965 1900

Child Abuse & Education Productions Association,
10070 King George Highway, Suite 101,
P.O. Box 183,
Surrey, B.C.
V3T 4W8   Tel:1 604 581 5116
In Quebec   Tel:1 514 585 1423

In New Zealand

Family Planning Association
214 Karangahape Road
Auckland 1   Tel: (09) 796 182

Help Foundation (Sexual Assault Victims)
1st Floor, 427 Queen Street
Auckland 1   Tel: Auckland (09) 399 185
                              South Auckland (09) 276 4076
                                 Male Help (09) 274 9784

Rape Crisis
63 Ponsonby Road
Auckland 2   Tel: (09) 764 404

Child Abuse Prevention Society Inc
Almorah Road
Epsom
Auckland 3   Tel: (09) 601 052

Although these are all Auckland phone numbers, these
people can of course give contact numbers throughout
the country, where available.

In Australia

Canberra Children's Services
(9am to 5pm)   Tel: (062) 462625

Sydney Child Protection and Family Crisis
(24 hours)   Tel:(02) 818 5555

Darwin Department for Community Development
                                    Tel: (089) 814 733

Brisbane Crisis Care
(24 hours)   Tel: (07) 224 6855

Adelaide Crisis Care
(24 hours)   Tel: (08) 272 1222

Hobart Department for Community Welfare, Crisis
Intervention
(24 hours)   Tel:(002) 302 529

Melbourne Protective Services for Children
(9am to 5pm)   Tel: (03) 309 5700

Perth Crisis Care
(24 hours)   Tel:(09) 321 4144
(toll free)   Tel: (008) 199 008

Lifeline and Rape Crisis Centres can be contacted
through your local directory.